THE ROYAL HORTICULTURAL SOCIETY
PRACTICAL GUIDES

CONTAINERS

THE ROYAL HORTICULTURAL SOCIETY
PRACTICAL GUIDES

CONTAINERS

Peter Robinson

DK

LONDON, NEW YORK, MUNICH, MELBOURNE, DELHI

PROJECT EDITOR Samantha Gray
ART EDITOR Rachael Parfitt

SERIES EDITOR Pamela Brown
SERIES ART EDITOR Stephen Josland

MANAGING EDITOR Louise Abbott
MANAGING ART EDITOR Lee Griffiths

DTP DESIGNER Matthew Greenfield

PRODUCTION MANAGER Patricia Harrington

This edition published in 2011
First published in Great Britain in 1999
by Dorling Kindersley Limited,
80 Strand, London WC2R 0RL

A Penguin Company

A CIP catalogue for this book is available from the British Library.
ISBN 978-0-7513-4724-1

Reproduced by Colourscan, Singapore
Printed and bound by Star Standard Industries, Singapore

Discover more at
www.dk.com

CONTENTS

GARDENING IN CONTAINERS

WHY CONTAINERS?

THERE CAN SCARCELY BE A YARD, balcony or garden, however big or small, that would not benefit from a container or two. Brimming with flowers or refreshing greenery, windowboxes, pots and planters help to soften urban landscapes dominated by bricks and concrete. They create leafy pools of interest outside back doors and basement flats, and bring colour and scent to patios and terraces, making them perfect places to relax and unwind.

CREATIVE BEGINNINGS

Just one striking plant in a single pot will brighten a windowsill or the corner of a yard, but a stylized line of matching plants or cascading mixture of flowers and foliage has real impact. Grouping plants in separate pots is the easiest way to create a display. You can cater for each plant's individual needs, varying watering and feeding regimes, adding and subtracting plants, and using different types of compost (*see p.55*). Mixed arrangements in large containers need more forethought but offer creative scope. Compost dries out less quickly in big pots but it is essential that all the plants share similar requirements for shade or sun, water and food, and grow at a similar pace if one is not to overrun the others.

◄ LAYERED EFFECT
A tiered arrangement that includes fuchsias, nasturtiums, begonias and pelargoniums makes maximum use of the space beneath a window. Staging can be bought ready-made; a lower display could easily be built up on stacked bricks.

▷ INSTANT SUNSHINE
A regimented row of dwarf sunflowers lights up a plain brick wall, albeit for a limited period.

CHOOSING CONTAINERS

Any container needs to be practical as well as decorative, so it is important to consider materials along with size, site and style when making your choice. It also helps if you know what you want to grow in it. The most successful combinations are those where plants suit their container and both

---

Wooden containers must be treated with a weatherproof preservative

---

container and plants suit their setting. Aim to choose a style that blends with your house or flat and garden, outdoor furniture and the standing surface, be it concrete, gravel, wooden decking or brick.

Terracotta harmonizes easily and develops an attractive weathered look (this can be speeded up by coating the outside of new pots with yogurt to attract algae and lichens). In warm weather, it tends to keep plant roots a little cooler than, say, plastic. On the minus side, large pots are heavy to move once planted and can be expensive.

Terracotta is breakable and can crack in frost (if this happens, a band of wire under the rim, twisted tight with pliers, usually keeps the pot in one piece and still functional). Since it is porous, clay will draw moisture from the compost which then evaporates from the outside of the pot; soaking new pots before planting reduces the problem. Plastic, on the other hand, is light, durable and inexpensive, but tall plants can make pots unstable. Compost, however, is less inclined to dry out.

FOLIAGE EFFECT
The aeonium (right), *adds an architectural dimension to a garden setting in summer. In cold areas it would need moving into a greenhouse or conservatory for winter. Conversely, the ornamental kale* (below), *with its matching pot, would enliven a dull corner from autumn into the new year.*

Subtle or Bold

Wood generally marries well with both plants and surroundings. It needs to be treated with a waterproof preservative in a natural shade or one of the attractive range of colours now available (*see p.33*). You can line the inside with polythene, punctured with drainage holes, or stand a plastic pot or trough inside. All containers need to be raised off the ground on feet or blocks, to allow water to drain; this is especially important for wood, to prevent the base from rotting.

Small trees and tall shrubs need sturdy, stable containers. Reconstituted stone pots are among the heaviest. If plants are tender and need moving into a greenhouse or conservatory for winter, use a trolley or a board fitted with wheels for transport.

Some of the cheaper, less attractive materials, or maybe containers that have passed their prime, can be transformed with a couple of coats of paint, a simple stencil or a mosaic of broken tiles (*see Creative Ideas, pp.25–29*). If you use strong colours, choose suitably bold plants that won't be outshone by their container.

△ TIME FOR MOSAIC
The slightly tender lavender, L. stoechas, is a good match for this mosaic pot. Hardier 'Hidcote' would make a suitable alternative.

▽ BASEMENT GREENERY
A classic example of the value of containers in an enclosed space without soil. Almost every centimetre of wall and floor is put to good use.

SITING AND GROUPING CONTAINERS

CONTAINERS GIVE YOU THE OPPORTUNITY to combine contrasting plants in a small area. Group displays extend the options because you can use plants that have different compost, watering and feeding needs. To emphasize contrast in foliage form, opt for containers of a similar material and colour. Single architectural specimens look best set apart. Use them as a focal point in the centre of a courtyard or to draw the eye to the end of a path or lawn.

RIGHT PLANT, RIGHT PLACE

Placing and arranging container plants needs the same sort of care that you would give to planting a bed or border. Plants in pots are more exposed to extremes of weather than those growing in the ground; their roots may overheat in summer or freeze in winter. In cold areas, be prepared to give plants that are not fully hardy winter protection (*see p.59*); in summer, the outer pots in a group will help to keep the

inner ones cooler. For hot sites choose plants that grow well in dry conditions, usually those with spiky or needle-like, furry or waxy, often grey leaves.

Flowers in strong primary colours, particularly reds, are most effective in strong light; pastel shades are often best kept away from full sun. Foliage colour is also affected by light intensity. Many variegated plants need sunshine to bring out the best coloration in their leaves.

FOCAL POINT
A spiky cordyline closes a vista. Make planting easy by using a plastic pot in the top of an Ali Baba jar, with some stones in the base to keep it stable. This makes the plant easy to move.

FRAGRANT REWARDS

Growing scented and aromatic plants in containers means that you can place them in just the right spot to appreciate them, near tables and chairs, for instance, or immediately by a door. In small courtyard areas, scents linger on warm afternoons and evenings, increasing the pleasure of sitting, eating and drinking outdoors.

Lilies make splendid container plants, but, if scent is all-important, check before buying since some have little or no smell.

> On summer evenings, the scent from windowsill plants can waft indoors

Heliotrope and dwarf tobacco plants (*Nicotiana*) are suitable for windowboxes, along with aromatic herbs such as thyme and marjoram. Shrubs provide some of the finest scents. For exoticism, angels' trumpets (*Brugmansia*) are hard to rival in summer, while the leaves of evergreen rosemary, lavender and myrtle remain aromatic all year. Place them where you can brush past and catch the benefit. Given the support of a wigwam of canes or hazel sticks or a wire or trellis obelisk, sweet peas can be grown in a large pot. They will need frequent watering and regular feeding.

▲ GROUP STRATEGY
The introduction of containerized grasses as a foreground to the broad-leaved hostas creates a display based on contrasting foliage shapes.

▼ COURTYARD COMPOSITION
The gentle colours of the tulips, pansies and pelargoniums and the natural textures of the trough and pots both harmonize with and enhance the backdrop of a grey stone wall.

MATCHING PLANTS WITH POTS

THERE IS AN ENORMOUS RANGE OF PLANTS that can be grown in containers, from summer bedding to small trees, provided the container is stable and there is room for plant roots. Containers enable you to grow plants that would not survive in your garden soil: rhododendrons, for example, which need acid conditions. In a tub you can use acid, ericaceous compost. It is easy, too, to improve drainage with extra grit for rock plants and Mediterranean herbs.

STYLE AND PURPOSE

Take advantage of a plant's natural habit of growth when matching it with its container. Give a trailing plant sufficient height to spill over the sides. Chimney pots and urns are ideal. Alternatively, stand a smaller pot on a small stack of bricks or another upturned pot. Most group displays are improved if you can set some of the plants at different levels. Trailing fuchsias, helichrysums, nasturtiums and lobelias can all be put to good use. These are also the sort of plants you need to soften the edges of a mixed planting in a large container. A mixture of different habits – upright and bushy, trailing or spreading – make any display more interesting whether planted in one or several separate containers.

Rock plants, small bulbs and carpeting herbs like thymes generally do not need deep root runs and suit shallow pots. Rosettes of sempervivums will thrive and multiply in as little as 8–10cm of compost.

Balance is all-important. Think about the shape any plant will develop when teaming it with its container. Too small a plant in too large a pot is likely to look silly. It is also unwise to give a plant more compost than its roots can possibly reach and which may become sodden and stale. While waiting for a newly planted shrub to grow to its full size, fill the space in a large container with annuals such as busy lizzies (*Impatiens*), pansies and mimulus. Or better still, pot the shrub on, year after year, gradually increasing the pot's size.

THE SHAPE OF THINGS
The garden, right, constructed entirely of raised beds and containers on different levels makes a fine setting for spiky foliage plants and trailing creepers. Similarly, a simple but stylish pot emphasizes the neat pincushion shape of the saxifrage below.

CUTTING EDGE
*Box plants have been
cleverly clipped into
shapes that work well
with their containers.
Choose containers
with uniform, muted
colours and textures
that do not detract
from the topiary.*

FLORA AND FAUNA
*Characterful birds,
and other animals,
can be created by
training small-leaved
ivies around a wire
frame (see p.62).
The results are more
rapid than by clipping
box or yew.*

THINKING BIG

For trees and shrubs that will be an
important part of the scene for many years,
perhaps the backbone of a grouping or a
specimen displayed in splendid isolation, it
is often worth investing in an especially
attractive planter or pot. Some plants and

> Topiary that needs years
> of dedicated clipping
> deserves a fine pot

containers make obvious partners. Beautiful
glazed ceramic pots suit oriental-looking
trees and shrubs such as Japanese maples,
bamboos and rhododendrons.

Unfortunately, the more valuable the pot
(and its plant) the greater the chance of it
being stolen and you may need to think
about some form of security, such as
threading a chain through the drainage
hole and padlocking it to a post or railing,
or even cementing the pot in place.

IDEAS FOR IMPROVISATION

THERE ARE MANY ALTERNATIVES to using purpose-made containers for plants. Virtually any object that can hold compost and be adapted with drainage holes may be transformed into a plant pot. Chimney pots, wicker baskets, hollowed-out tree trunks, wellington boots, wheelbarrows, ceramic sinks, galvanized buckets and old bird cages are in many cases not as costly as shop-bought containers and will add a sense of originality to your garden.

CHARACTERFUL CONTAINERS

Chimney pots are particularly useful for introducing height to a container grouping. Their narrow shape also makes them very suitable for limited spaces. Instead of filling the entire depth with compost, insert a smaller pot in the top, as for the Ali Baba jar (*see p.10*); support it if necessary by part-filling the chimney pot with bricks or stones. Alternatively, fill the chimney pot to half its depth with a good drainage material, such as hardcore or cobblestones with pea gravel in between, then add potting compost to just below the rim. Tall containers, including chimney pots and galvanized metal florists' buckets, look best displaying plants such as trailing fuchsias or petunias which can spill attractively down the sides.

If you are inventive, you can also make decorative containers from inexpensive salvage materials, such as ceramic tiles, terracotta ridging tiles or large terracotta drainpipes. You may have such materials left over from building projects, or you can

≫ CHIMNEY POT DISPLAY
A chimney pot is an ideal container for the tender fuchsia 'Annabel', which should be moved to a frost-free place in winter.

▼ CONTAINERS FROM CLAY TILES
Containers made from sections of clay tiles combine subtle colours that offset the vibrant pelargonium blooms.

Potting compost fills only the upper part of the chimney pot, inside a smaller pot or over a base layer of drainage material

An underplanting of *Lobelia erinus* 'White Cascade' trails over the edges of the pot

◀ VEGETABLE RACK
*A vegetable rack
lined with moss and
an inner layer of
polythene provides
ample space for
compost in which
to grow plants, here
including dark-leaved
basil, thyme, curled
parsley and scented
pelargonium.*

▼ HOLLOW LOG
*A contrast in colour
and habit is provided
by* Heuchera
'Palace Purple' *and*
Dryopteris *planted in
a hollowed-out log.
Make sure that there
are drainage holes in
the base of the
container.*

obtain them inexpensively from a salvage
yard. Where necessary, join pieces together
with mortar, making sure that any large
area of mortar is inside the container.

All sorts of objects can make surprisingly
effective containers. For example, a vegetable
rack can be lined with moss with an inner

Make sure that all
improvised containers
have drainage holes

layer of polythene. Cut holes in the base of
the polythene for drainage and make slits in
the sides through which you can insert
young plants in the same way as planting up
a hanging basket. A hollowed-out tree trunk
can be turned into an attractive container, or
pieces of bark-covered timber can be nailed
together to make a trough. Stand timber
containers on wedges and use a compost
that allows rapid drainage (*see pp.54–55*).

TREES, SHRUBS AND CLIMBERS

GROWING WOODY PLANTS IN CONTAINERS gives a sense of permanence and structure to a paved area, while the plants themselves can influence the style of the garden, creating a formal, informal or even sub-tropical effect. By matching an elegantly shaped or handsomely textured container with a boldly sculptural small tree or shrub, you can create a stunning focal point. The range of plants you can grow is much greater if you are able to give them some protection in winter.

SCREENING AND PRIVACY

Evergreen trees, shrubs and climbers grown in containers will soften the appearance of walls, fences and other hard surfaces all year round, and help to increase privacy. For sculptural form, grow evergreens with boldly shaped leaves, such as × *Fatshedera lizei*, fatsia, palm-like cordylines and *Cycas revoluta*. Exotic and eye-catching, the last two need careful placing and, in cold climates, will need to be moved into a greenhouse or conservatory for winter. In enclosed town gardens you may want to increase the sense of light and air with a delicate-leaved Japanese maple (*Acer palmatum*) or a variegated aralia.

A CORNER DISPLAY
The catkins of this Kilmarnock willow (Salix caprea 'Kilmarnock') *appear like large droplets from a fountain over the cool blue container and the underplanting of* Helleborus argutifolius. *Surrounding the container are* Helleborus foetidus, *the striking foliage of* Arum italicum *and a hebe, bringing this corner to life in late winter.*

A PERFECT MATCH
The oriental effect of this blue-glazed container and the pebble mulch complement the purple-leaved Japanese maple. The pebbles have practical value as well, keeping the roots shaded and cool and helping to conserve moisture.

COLOUR AND SCENT

One of the pleasures of container planting is the ease with which you can introduce flower or foliage colour to areas that might otherwise lack interest. Silver-leaved shrubs, such as *Convolvulus cneorum*, help to cool down sunny patios, and both foliage and flowers of a variegated abutilon have a refreshing quality. Make the most of trees and shrubs with scented flowers or leaves – lavender and rosemary, for instance – by siting them near a sitting area. Since this is likely to be the most sheltered part of the garden, it will also suit myrtle and bay, which both need protection from cold winds that can scorch their leaves.

YEAR-ROUND INTEREST

Many sculptural plants look even more effective in winter than during the summer, for example, the formal contours of a geometrically clipped box (*Buxus*) or yew (*Taxus*). Japanese maples come into their own again at this time of year with their exquisite tracery of fine branches, and the bare twisting stems of the corkscrew hazel, *Corylus avellana* 'Contorta', and *Salix* 'Erythroflexuosa' also have great impact when they are grown in containers. Ivies, such as yellow-variegated 'Goldheart' or curly-leaved 'Cristata', can be used to enliven gloomy corners or camouflage unsightly vertical surfaces. In summer,

Balance tall trees and shrubs with handsome, sturdy containers

some forms of greenery can be just as interesting as flowers. Try introducing some sound with the gentle rustle of a bamboo such as *Sasa palmata* f. *nebulosa*. Given a reasonably sheltered spot, its broad, glossy leaves can look splendid all year.

FLOWERS FOR CONTAINERS

MAKE THE MOST OF THE WONDERFUL RANGE of tender perennials and annuals that actually thrive in scorching sunlight to bring flower colour to parts of the garden where woody plants would soon show signs of suffering. By contrast, the deep shade caused by buildings or high fences can be perfect for many herbaceous perennials, and for many lilies. Use bulbs, such as small narcissus and crocus or bright tulips, to extend the flowering season in spring and autumn.

EXUBERANT DISPLAYS

The ever-expanding range of summer bedding on offer as small plantlets or plugs in garden centres and catalogues makes it easy to put together stunning combinations without the bother of sowing seed, pricking out and hardening off. Many of these plants have been bred specially for container-

▲ HOT COLOURS FOR A SUNNY SITE
A terracotta pot holds a vibrant display of red-and gold-flowering plants, including cosmos, Rudbeckia *'Rustic Dwarfs' and 'Marmalade',* helichrysum *and* Santolina chamaecyparissus.

growing and are both compact and free-flowering. Although often on sale in spring, buy them early only if you have a greenhouse where you can bring them on. Do not be tempted to plant them outside until all danger of frost is past.

For continuous flowering, deadhead plants regularly and feed occasionally with a high-potash feed such as tomato fertilizer. A lot of annuals and bedding plants such as gerberas, pelargoniums, osteospermums, salvias and salpiglossis need sun to produce their best flowers, but lobelia, busy lizzies (*Impatiens*), *Begonia semperflorens*, pansies and tobacco plants (*Nicotiana*) all flower

> Trailing lobelias create a curtain of flowering stems for a windowbox

well in light shade. For a plant that will still flower through a dull, damp summer, petunias make the best choice, with a wide range of flower colours – hot or cool, dashingly striped or prettily veined.

PERENNIALS FOR POTS

Use large tubs to group perennials or, easier to arrange, plant them singly in smaller containers. Striking single plantings include agapanthus, with elegant large blue or white flowerheads, and variegated hostas for decorative foliage and flowers.

Many herbaceous perennials, particularly woodland species such as heucheras and

⚘ PORTABLE PLANTS
Small containers allow you to move plants like tender Eucomis bicolor *outside in summer, then back into a cold frame for winter protection.*

⚘ SIMPLE BUT DRAMATIC
A group of variegated 'Keizerskroon' tulips shows the impact that can be made by planting a single variety.

tiarellas, are shade tolerant. Set them off with perennial foliage plants with a distinctive shape and growth habit, such as ornamental grasses and ferns, which thrive in shade. Most perennials provide summer interest only, but there are a few exceptions, such as liriope and bergenia, with evergreen foliage as well as attractive flowers in autumn and spring respectively.

BEST WAYS FOR GROWING BULBS

In large containers, bulbs can be planted in layers (*see p.57*) with annuals growing above for instant colour. Often, however, they are best grown in a container of their own. Tulips, for instance, make a striking display; in pots they are best grown for one season only and then planted in the garden after flowering, if possible. Lilies are irresistible and make excellent container plants, but their displays are brief and they, too, are best grown in separate pots.

⚘ COOL WHITES TO THRIVE IN SUNSHINE
This sun-loving mixture of white petunias and Helichrysum *'Roundabout' takes on a luminous quality in dusky evening light.*

FRUIT, VEGETABLES AND HERBS

MOST HERBS MAKE IDEAL CONTAINER PLANTS, their aromatic leaves scenting windowsills and patios (*see overleaf*). Fruit and vegetables demand time and care, requiring regular watering and feeding – a liquid fertilizer is easiest to apply. You will never produce mammoth crops but at least they can go straight from plant to plate. In cool climates, citrus trees will be ornamental rather than productive; curly lettuce or tiers of ripening strawberries will fulfil both roles.

FRUIT IN CONTAINERS

Fruit in containers can be included in an ornamental garden scheme more easily than vegetables. In a sunny courtyard or patio, you can create a Mediterranean effect by growing figs and citrus trees in pots, although they will need to be protected from frost in winter in a greenhouse or conservatory.

Consider what types of containers will best suit what you want to grow. Fruit trees need large containers that can hold enough compost to act as a buffer for roots in dry conditions. Strawberry pots look decorative and are a space-saving way to grow

> On a patio, you may get to the strawberry crop before the birds

strawberry plants, provided all the fruit receives sufficient sun to ripen. You may need to turn the pot from time to time. Tiny alpine strawberries do well in light shade and provide small but delicious pickings. Add extra grit to compost for strawberries, especially in the tiered, purpose-designed pots, to aid water penetration. Regular watering is essential while fruit is swelling.

VEGETABLES IN CONTAINERS

The best vegetables for containers are the shallow-rooted, compact, quick-maturing varieties. To create a mini-potager effect, plant more than one type of vegetable in a

MEDITERRANEAN-STYLE CITRUS
A lemon tree growing in an elegant terracotta pot looks wonderful on a sunny patio. You will need to move it into a conservatory or greenhouse for protection from frost in winter.

large container, combining, for instance, frilly-leaved lettuces such as 'Lollo Rossa' and feathery-topped carrots. Growing a combination of plants can help to ward off pests, which are less attracted to mixed scents than strong, single ones.

If you have a really sunny, sheltered corner, it is fun to try some of the colourful varieties of aubergine, chilli and sweet pepper. They are tender and need a long growing season to produce anything edible, but some seed suppliers offer an exciting range, occasionally as small plants.

⚞ A MINI-POTAGER
A wooden trough filled with a combination of red cabbages and nasturtiums creates a mini-potager effect and allows the occasional plundering of leaves for summer salads.

⚟ STRAWBERRY CASCADE
Terracotta pots, built up one inside the other with room between for compost and roots, create planting tiers that can be filled with a mixture of herbs and alpine strawberries.

SUITABLE VEGETABLES

FOR SUN AND SHELTER

Aubergine Small-fruited types
Chillies Compact varieties, e.g.'Apache'
Tomatoes Fast-ripening, small-fruited types
Peppers Compact varieties, e.g. 'Redskin'

FOR LIGHT SHADE

French beans Dwarf, can be purple-podded
Runner beans Need a large tub plus wigwam of canes
Lettuce Decorative types, e.g.'Lollo Rossa'
Carrots Stump-rooted varieties

GROWING HERBS

The great advantage of planting edible herbs in pots is that you can position them in a convenient spot near to the house. Placing a herb container by the back door, for example, will allow you to water the plants and gather foliage easily.

Make sure that mixed species chosen for the same pot all enjoy the same conditions. Many herbs are of Mediterranean origin and require plenty of sunshine and good drainage to thrive and survive wet winters. Thyme, marjoram, rosemary, basil, bay and sage all need sun, which also improves their flavour. Rosemary and bay need shelter, too. Chives, parsley, chervil and mint grow well in light shade; give mint a container of its own or it will overrun any neighbours. Suitable composts include John Innes No.2 or a loamless compost. For Mediterranean herbs, add some sharp sand or grit.

◄ CULINARY TRIO
A standard bay tree with an underplanting of thyme and parsley provides the necessary ingredients for a "bouquet garni" to add piquancy to the cooking pot.

▲ AROMATIC ARRANGEMENT
A strawberry pot can be filled with attractive foliage herbs, such as purple and variegated sages, 'Silver Posie' thyme and marjoram.

▼ PUNGENT PARTNERS
A neat display combines basil and unrelated basil thyme (Acinos arvensis). Basil needs frequent harvesting or stems become lanky.

A mophead bay tree needs regular clipping whether bought as a standard or trained from a small plant (see p.61)

CREATIVE IDEAS FOR CONTAINERS

STENCILLED MOTIF P.26

IT IS EASY TO TRANSFORM terracotta or plastic containers by decorating them with paint or stencilled patterns (*see pp.24–26*), perhaps to complement a colour theme in your garden. For a really dazzling effect, cover pots with mosaic, using pieces of broken tile, even glass beads, pieces of mirror or seashells (*see pp.27–29*). A windowbox provides welcome colour through the seasons.

You can make boxes to fit your windows perfectly and then use a paint finish, such as verdigris or crackle glaze, to give them the patina of age (*see pp.30–35*). Or, you may prefer to use wooden mouldings to create a decorative panelled or ribbed effect (*see pp.36–37*). Before planting, it is important that the box is secured to the sill (*see pp.38–39*).

CRACKLE-GLAZE PAINT P.35

With a little woodworking skill, you can construct wooden planters that are both distinctive and stylish (*see pp.40–47*). Neither of the projects here requires specialist tools or tricky carpentry joints.

Old stone troughs add a sense of time to a garden and form a pleasing setting for plants. But they are costly to buy. The solution is to make inexpensive "fake"

CLASSIC WOODEN PLANTER P.44

troughs that are difficult to tell apart from the real thing. Two projects (*see pp.48–53*) show how to coat crates with natural-looking hypertufa or an especially tough cement mix, which can be painted to give a colourful, contemporary feel.

ALPINE
TROUGH P.52

DECORATED POTS

FLOWERPOTS OF ALL SHAPES AND SIZES offer tremendous scope for adding decoration. Apply a colourwash to brighten a dull corner, stencil on shells, stars – whatever takes your fancy and suits your planting scheme (*see overleaf*). Mosaic (*see p.27*) is more ambitious but looks superb teamed with dramatic yuccas and other bold foliage plants. You can transform utilitarian plastic and, now that factory-made terracotta has become so much more affordable, take the opportunity to experiment and make pots that are unique to your garden.

DISTRESSING TERRACOTTA

Give new terracotta pots a mellow, antique look by applying two colours, then rubbing patches of one away. Use water-based paint, preferably with a fairly chalky texture. The emulsion formulated for the distressed look and other special effects – often found in art or decorating shops – works well.

YOU NEED:

MATERIALS
- Terracotta pot
- Water-based emulsion paint in two colours
- Exterior matt varnish
- White spirit

TOOLS
- Paint brush
- Wire wool in fine and coarse grades

TWO-COLOUR EFFECT

1 **Paint the pot** with the first, base colour, including inside the rim to just below the planting level. Leave to dry.

2 **Apply the second colour.** You can water it down slightly over areas that are to be rubbed off in Step 3. Leave to dry.

3 **Rub away** some patches of the top coat of paint to reveal the base coat, using first coarse and then fine grade wire wool Blur edges as much as possible.

4 **Brush off all dust** then apply a coat of exterior varnish for a weatherproof finish. Matt varnish loses its glossiness when dry.

◀ SHADES OF SUMMER *Pinks, greens and blues harmonize well with both foliage and flowers.*

STENCILLING PATTERNS

If you are new to stencilling, choose a fairly simple motif, one that does not require intricate cutting-out. The texture of clay provides an attractive background in itself, but a plastic pot, as shown below, needs to be painted first. When making the stencil, cut away all the excess card so that you are left with the narrowest of borders around the design. You can then stick the stencil closely to the pot and so avoid spoiling the edge of the pattern.

USING SIMPLE MOTIFS

YOU NEED:

MATERIALS
- Flexible card
- Clay flowerpot
- Emulsion or acrylic paint
- Scrap paper
- Exterior varnish
- White spirit

TOOLS
- Pencil
- Craft knife
- Masking tape
- Sponge
- Paint brush

1 Draw or trace the design onto a piece of flexible card and carefully cut it out using a craft knife. Protect work surfaces.

2 Stick the stencil in place with the tape, stretching the card as taut as possible to prevent any paint from seeping underneath.

3 Dab on the paint using a sponge. Get rid of any excess paint first on some scrap paper. When dry, peel off the stencil (*see inset*) and varnish the pot, as on the previous page.

USING PLASTIC POTS

Apply an oil-based undercoat first to create a suitable surface for paint to adhere to, then a base, background coat of emulsion. Stencil on the motif in the same way as above, but remove the tape as gently as possible to avoid pulling off the base coat along with it. Varnish as before.

A mollusc has been stencilled onto a base coat of slate-blue emulsion. The rim is painted pink to match it

MAKING MOSAIC

Use mosaic to cover cheap or cracked terracotta or even thick, rigid plastic. The pattern can be as flamboyant or subtle as you want but, for a first attempt, avoid intricacy and choose the kind of random design shown here.

The spiky silhouette of *Yucca gloriosa* 'Variegata' suits the mosaic pattern

YOU NEED:

MATERIALS
- Flowerpot
- Drawing paper
- Tiles or old china
- Water-resistant combined tile adhesive and grout
- Emulsion or acrylic paint

TOOLS
- Ruler and pencil
- Hammer
- Cloth or newspaper
- Protective eye goggles
- Rubber gloves
- Pincers or tile nippers
- Tile file
- Flexible filling knife
- Spatula and sponge
- Paint brush

PLANT PARTNERS
Bold pots call for bold plants. Those with architectural shapes, such as this yucca, are ideal (take care, the leaves are very sharp). Phormiums, agaves or succulents such as aeoniums would also be a good choice for a sunny corner. The shapes of these hot-climate plants suit the Mediterranean feeling of mosaic.

PLANNING THE DESIGN

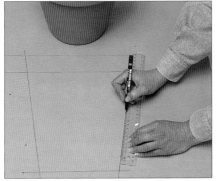

1 **Measure and mark out** the shape of the pot, including the depth of the rim. You can do this in segments of halves or thirds.

2 **Place the tiles** between cloth or paper, to stop fragments flying, and smash them with a hammer. For extra safety wear goggles.

SHAPING AND FIXING THE PIECES

1 **Lay out the pieces** in your chosen pattern, using pincers to fashion the shapes and nip corners. Start from the top, laying pieces with a glazed edge at the rim for a smooth edge.

2 **Use a tile file** to remove any jagged edges and shape the pieces further. Keep your eyes protected with goggles while you are nipping or filing pieces of mosaic.

4 **Spread the grout** all over the surface of the mosaic, working it well into the joints between the pieces. Do not worry about getting it over the tiles – it will wipe off. (You can add coloured dyes to the grout if you want it to blend or contrast with the mosaic.)

PRACTICAL TIPS

- Thin tiles are easiest to use. Keep to ceramics of an even thickness.
- Avoid tiles with a crackle glaze as they break with especially jagged edges.
- Keep the mosaic pieces fairly small.
- A combined adhesive/grout simplifies the job, but you can use separate formulations.

3 **Stick the mosaic pieces** onto the pot, smearing the undersides thickly with tile adhesive using a flexible knife. Keep them in the arranged pattern as you transfer them one by one from paper to pot. Leave to set.

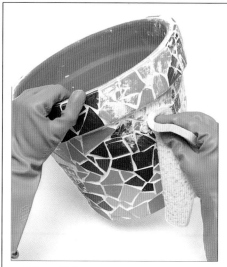

5 **Wipe off the excess grout** with a damp sponge or cloth before it hardens. When it has fully set, you can buff up the surface of the mosaic using a dry sponge or cloth.

6 **Paint the inside rim,** using a colour that suits the mosaic, to just below the compost level. This improves the finished look and hides any smudges of adhesive and grout.

ALTERNATIVE MATERIALS FOR MOSAICS

With a little inventiveness all sorts of materials can be put to good use. Some will fare better than others in harsh weather. The glass tesserae, below right, made specially for mosaic, are frost-resistant. A coat of varnish will give shells a longer life.

◀MIRROR
Rather than letting them bring you bad luck, use broken pieces to add a surreal touch, but handle them carefully.

GLASS NUGGETS ▶
These are sold for arranging in coloured layers in jars, but are excellent for mosaic work.

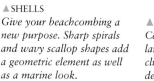

▲SHELLS
Give your beachcombing a new purpose. Sharp spirals and wavy scallop shapes add a geometric element as well as a marine look.

▲BEADS
Ceramic or glass, small or large, use beads singly or in clusters to add interesting detail to a design.

▼TESSERAE
You can find a wide range of colours in craft shops and specialist mosaic suppliers.

WINDOWBOXES

A WINDOW WITHOUT A WINDOWBOX is a wasted opportunity for anyone who likes plants. Nor do the creative possibilities begin and end with deciding what to grow. The box itself can be decorated in many ways. Give it a rustic look or an air of urban sophistication with paint or ornamental wood finishes (*see pp.34–37*). Then, to create an effective planting scheme, experiment with combinations of upright and trailing plants and those with attractive foliage.

MAKING A WOODEN WINDOWBOX

Simple troughs made of weatherproofed wood can be planted up direct, or used to hold pots. This windowbox has been designed for a ledge 100×20cm, but the same method of construction can be used to suit any size. Remember that the bigger the box, the more securely it must be fixed to the sill (*see pp.38–39*).

PRACTICAL TIPS

• If altering the dimensions of the box, make sure that it will still be deep enough for plant roots (for most plants, at least 19cm).
• Smooth all rough, sawn timber edges with sandpaper before you start.
• When drilling, always put a spare offcut of wood underneath to protect the work surface.

YOU NEED:

MATERIALS
For this project, use wood of 2cm thickness. The timber measurements are all for finished, planed wood.
• 2 side panels 96.5×19cm
• 2 end panels 17×17cm
• Base 96.5×17cm
• 30 size 8, 2in (5cm) screws plus a few extra
• Wood filler
• Your choice of materials to protect and decorate the box (*see pp.33–37*)

TOOLS
• Pencil
• Tape measure
• Drill, preferably electric
• 4mm drill bit
• Countersink
• 13mm drill bit, for drainage holes
• Screwdriver

POSITIONING THE END PANELS

1 **Lay the base** flat on the workbench or table and, holding each of the small end panels in position against it, mark a line on the base along their inside edge.

2 **Mark, then drill** 3 evenly spaced holes for screws at each end of the base, using the 4mm bit. Rest each end of the base on spare offcuts of wood to keep it level and protect the work surface from the drill. Use a countersink (*see inset*) to make a shallow depression so that the screw head will lie just below the surface of the wood.

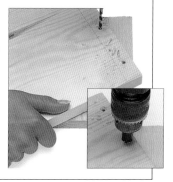

◀ HANGING GARDENS *Trailing fuchsias, pelargoniums and a calceolaria create a cascade of colour.*

CONSTRUCTING THE BOX

3 Screw one end panel in place; you can use the other end panel, as here, for support. Screw the remaining end panel onto the other end of the base in the same way.

PRACTICAL TIPS

• For extra strength, glue joints with wood adhesive before screwing if you prefer, but it is not essential.

• When screwing one piece of wood to another, avoid any chance of the wood splitting by making a small "starter" hole in the second piece first, using a bradawl or a very fine drill.

4 Lay each of the side panels flat on the workbench in turn, and place the ends-and-base construction on them, marking around its inner edge.

5 Mark screw positions at equal intervals along the marked-off area, placing 3 up each of the side edges and 4 along the bottom edge. Bear in mind that the screws near the corners must be well clear of the joint.

6 At each marked position, drill and countersink screw holes on each of the long side panels. Screw the side panels to the base and end panels in order to complete the basic construction of the box.

HIDING SCREWS AND DRILLING DRAINAGE HOLES

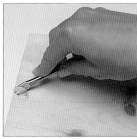

2 **Turn the box** upside down and drill holes in the base of the box for drainage, using the 13mm bit. A box of these dimensions will need at least 6 holes.

1 **Fill in** the countersunk screw holes with wood filler to cover the screw heads. Make the filling slightly proud then sand it smooth and level when dry.

PROTECTING AND PRESERVING THE WOOD

Wood must be protected from the effects of damp compost within and rain and sun without, so it is essential to use an exterior-quality product to weatherproof it. Always treat both the inside and outside of any wooden container with preservative. You can use oil-based paint over primer but it will need to be renewed regularly. More decorative paint finishes include crackle glaze and "verdigris" effects (*see overleaf*).

PRACTICAL TIPS
• For extra protection, line the inside with polythene punctured with drainage holes, or stand a plastic box inside to make it easy to swap planting schemes whenever necessary.
• Stand the windowbox on wedges or feet so that water drains freely. Use a tray to catch surplus water and prevent it from dripping onto balconies or pavements beneath.

BRIGHT HARMONY
Exterior preservatives, designed to let wood grain show through, come in an attractive range of soft colours as well as natural wood shades.

"FORGET-ME-NOT"   "IRIS BLUE"   "SAGE GREEN"   "SUNFLOWER"

Apply preservative evenly and, if possible, in the direction of the grain

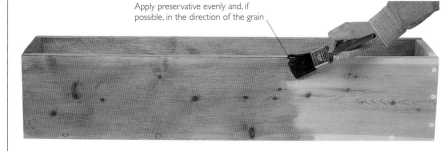

DECORATIVE PAINT FINISHES

It is easy to give a "designer" look to simple wooden containers by using craft paints to add colour and texture. You can apply these paint finishes to any wooden container, including the planters on pages 40–47. Always apply clear exterior varnish over paint finishes to protect and seal them.

CREATING A VERDIGRIS EFFECT

YOU NEED:

MATERIALS
- Wood primer and undercoat, or an all-in-one product
- Olive green acrylic or emulsion paint
- Small pots of mint green, blue-green and black acrylic paint
- Bronze or copper gilt cream
- Clear exterior matt varnish

TOOLS
- Paint brush
- Stencil brush
- Scrap paper
- Brush cleaner

1 Paint the bare wood with primer and undercoat. Using an all-in-one, fast-drying product is a good way to save time.

2 Apply an even coat of olive green paint. Use long brush strokes and work in the same direction as the grain. Leave to dry.

3 Dip the stencil brush into the mint green paint and dab off the excess onto paper. Stipple on the colour and leave to dry.

4 Stipple on the blue-green paint, applying it sparingly to create random concentrations of colour. Allow the paint to dry.

5 Mix some black paint with the blue-green to make a dark shade. Use it to work in smudges of deeper colour to create a naturalistic effect. Leave to dry.

6 Apply tiny patches of bronze or copper gilt cream with your fingertip. Seal with up to 3 coats of varnish. Give 2 coats of varnish to the inside of the box.

PRACTICAL TIPS
- Cover mistakes with undercoat and have another go.
- Choose good-quality brushes for the best finish.
- Most DIY superstores now stock small ranges of craft paints.

USING CRACKLE GLAZE

YOU NEED:

MATERIALS
• Wood primer and undercoat
• Base coat of acrylic paint (*here gold*)
• Crackle glaze
• Top coat of acrylic or emulsion paint (*here olive*)
• Clear exterior varnish, preferably with a matt or semi-gloss finish

TOOLS
• Paint brush
• Brush cleaner

1 **Prime and undercoat** the wood, then brush on gold paint (*above*). Brush in the same direction as the wood grain and allow to dry.

2 **Apply one thick coat** or two thin coats of crackle glaze. (The top layer of paint will not crackle if there is not enough glaze.) Leave to dry.

3 **Paint on a coat** of olive green, using long, even brush strokes and keeping the brush loaded with plenty of paint. Allow to dry. As the paint dries it will shrink and crackle.

4 **Apply up to 3 coats** of exterior varnish to seal the paint and the wood underneath it to protect them from the weather. Then apply 2 coats of varnish to the inside.

A SUBTLE PLANTING
The green and gold crackle glaze on the windowbox perfectly complements this sophisticated green and golden-yellow planting scheme, with the oval-shaped leaves of the hosta contrasting with the divided fern fronds. You could position this windowbox to brighten up a sunless spot, because this combination of plants will thrive in shade.

Mimulus luteus (Monkey musk)

Polystichum setiferum Divisilobum Group

Asplenium scolopendrium Cristatum Group

Hosta ventricosa var. aureomaculata

The crackle effect reveals the gold paint beneath the olive green

DECORATIVE WOODEN FINISHES

You can add interest to a plain box by decorating the surface with strips of wooden moulding, mitred and tacked to the front of the box (*below*), to look like panelling. Lengths of beading give a ribbed effect (*see facing page*); you could stain or paint this box in stripes of alternate colours (*see p.33*). Estimate the amount of moulding or beading required before starting either project. A weatherproof preservative needs to be applied inside and out.

CREATING A SIMPLE PANELLED EFFECT

YOU NEED:

MATERIALS
• Length of moulding
• 20mm galvanized pins
(Lengths and quantities required depend on the size of the windowbox)

TOOLS
• Tape measure
• Pencil
• Mitre box
• Panel saw
• Hammer
• Nail punch

1 **Mark out a rectangle** for the moulding's outer edge on the front of the box. Measure the long and the short sides, and mark out 2 of each on the outer edge of the moulding.

2 **Use a mitre box** to cut each of the 4 pieces of moulding at each end, making sure that the angles slant inwards from your mark to the inner edge of the moulding.

3 **Position the moulding** on the windowbox and place the pins in a groove of the moulding. Then hammer in the pins using a nail punch to hide their heads in the groove.

FINAL FLOURISH
Paint or preservative is essential to protect the wood – and can complement flower and foliage colours.

Ballota pseudodictamnus

Stachys lanata

Verbena 'Imagination'

Trifolium repens 'Purpurascens'

Sutera cordata 'Snowflake'

ADDING STRIPS OF BEADING

YOU NEED:

MATERIALS
• Length of 22mm half-round beading
• Length of 12×32mm doorstop to use as capping
• 20mm galvanized pins
(Lengths and quantities depend on windowbox size)

TOOLS
• Mitre box
• Panel saw
• Drill and fine drill bit
• Hammer

1 **Cut the beading** into lengths the same depth as the windowbox, using a mitre box to ensure 90° angles.

2 **Drill a fine hole** near each end of all the pieces to stop them splitting when tacking in place. Drill onto an offcut.

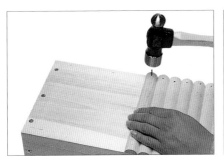

3 **Lay the pieces of beading** in a row along the front of the box. Adjust the spacing across the width if necessary so that the beading fits exactly, and tack it in place. Also tack 2–3 pieces at the front of each end.

4 **To cut the capping,** measure first from the front edge of the beading to the back of the box. When measuring the long sides, include the end beading. Cut the 4 pieces with 45° angled ends (*see Step 2, facing page*).

5 **Lay the capping** around the top of the box. Position all 4 pieces before fixing, as they might well need adjusting. Tack them in place with more pins. Finish the box by applying paint or preservative as desired.

PRACTICAL TIPS
• As fine drill bits have a tendency to break very easily, for Step 2 you can instead nip the head off one of the galvanized pins with pincers and use the pin in the drill as a bit.
• For a very rustic, chunky effect, you could also cover the front of a basic windowbox with log roll. This is available from garden centres in varying lengths and sizes.

FIXING WINDOWBOXES IN POSITION

Different styles of window call for different methods of fixing. You can use brackets (*see p.30*) under casement windows that open outwards. The box must be secure, especially important if overlooking a pavement. On sloping sills (20cm front to back minimum), wedges will hold the box level; for added safety, run strong wire around the front attached to vine eyes fixed to the wall. Use a tray to catch any water that may drip and cause a nuisance.

MAKING WEDGES FOR A SLOPING SILL

YOU NEED:

MATERIALS
• Wood offcut, 30mm narrower than windowbox and top 2 corners cut at right angles
• Wood preservative

TOOLS
• Small spirit level
• Tape measure
• Pencil • Set square
• Vice or other clamping device
• Panel saw
• Hammer
• Panel pins

1 To assess the slope of the windowsill, lay a small spirit level on the sill, from the inner to the outer edge, and raise it until it is completely level.

2 Measure and note the gap between the spirit level and the front of the windowsill. This gives you the measurement for the thick end of the wedge.

3 Mark this measurement down one side of the offcut and join with a thick line (the saw blade width) to the other corner to make the shape of the wedge.

4 Mark out a second identical wedge on the other side of the diagonal line and then cut out both wedges. Treat with the same preservative as the windowbox.

5 Using panel pins, tack the wedges onto the base of the box, at least 20cm from each end.

SECURING A BOX ON A WINDOWSILL

YOU NEED:

MATERIALS
- Mirror plates
- Screws
- Hooks

TOOLS
- Tape measure
- Pencil
- Bradawl
- Screwdriver

1 **Measure the width** of the window surround. Halve this measurement and mark it on the ends of the box to give the position of the centre of the mirror plates.

2 **Hold the mirror plates** in place on the windowbox. Start holes with a bradawl to stop the wood from splitting, then screw in position (*see inset*).

3 **Rest the box** on the sill and mark the position of each hook on the window surround, using the hook itself.

4 **Screw the hooks** into the window surround, and lift the box into position on the windowsill, slotting the holes in the mirror plates over the hooks. It is usually easier to plant up the windowbox once it is in place on the sill.

PLANTING UP
Making your own windowbox means that it will fit the sill exactly and the display of plants can extend to the full width of the window. Here, pink and plum-coloured pansies and ornamental cabbages have been chosen for a winter arrangement that also suits the colour of the box. Variegated ivy helps to soften the edges.

WOODEN PLANTERS

EVEN THE SIMPLEST SQUARE WOODEN PLANTER is expensive to buy, but if you have a knack for DIY – and an eye for three-dimensional jigsaw puzzles – planters really are easy to make. The two projects here require neither complicated carpentry joints nor specialist tools, and if you ask your timber supplier to cut the wood to length it will greatly speed up the job.

MAKING A PLAIN BOX PLANTER

This planter (*left*) is constructed in layers, each one screwed to the one beneath. The layers consist of 2 long side pieces and 2 slightly shorter ones. As the layers are built up, the pieces are alternated – long over short, short over long – so that the corners overlap and the planter is held firmly together. Position screws carefully so that you do not try to fix one into another below it.

YOU NEED:

MATERIALS
- 18 side pieces 45×4.5×4.5cm
- 18 side pieces 36×4.5×4.5cm
- 2 base battens 36×2×2cm
- 2 base battens 32×2×2cm
- 2 base boards 36×14×2cm
- 1 base board 36×7.5×2cm
- 4 pieces of capping 48×7×2cm
- 4 blocks for the feet 4.5×4.5×4.5cm

(These measurements are for finished, planed wood.)

TOOLS
- Electric drill
- 4mm drill bit
- 13mm drill bit (for drainage holes only)
- Panel saw
- 80 size 8, 3in (7.5cm) screws
- 30 size 7, 1¼in (3.2cm) screws
- Mitre box
- Screwdriver • Set square
- Pencil and tape measure
- Countersink
- Wood filler

HOW THE PARTS FIT TOGETHER

The pieces are fixed in place with screws

Short side piece

Long side piece

Alternate layers of short and long pieces

Cubes of wood raise the planter off the ground

SIMPLE PLANTER
The finished size of this planter is 48×48×47cm, but you can make whatever size of planter you prefer.

◄ COOL SIMPLICITY *Tall flower stems of agapanthus and galtonia are balanced by a large planter.*

STARTING THE PLANTER

1 **Drill 4 holes,** using a 4mm bit, in 2 long side pieces – one at each end and 2 evenly spaced in between – and 2 holes in 2 short side pieces, each a third of the way from the end.

2 **Set out 2 long and 2 short** undrilled side pieces to form a square, checking with a set square that they are at right angles. These pieces form the first layer of the planter.

Long side pieces are placed over short side pieces

3 **Place the drilled side pieces** exactly on top of the first layer, long over short, short over long, and fix in place using 3in screws. This is the basic assembly method.

4 **Drill, then screw** the base battens to the inside lower edge of the first layer, using 1¼in screws.

BUILDING UP THE SIDES

6 Mitre the corners on the capping at a 45° angle using a mitre box. Make each piece 48cm on the longer, outer edge. Drill and countersink holes either end and in the centre.

7 Screw the pieces of capping in place using 1¼in screws. The capping should overhang the sides of the planter by 1.5cm but check that all 4 pieces make an exact fit before fixing the screws.

5 Build up the sides by repeating step 3, first drilling holes in the side pieces and continuing to place long pieces above short and short above long, until all are used. On the top layer, use only 2 screws in each piece.

9 Make a couple of drainage holes in each of the base boards using the 13mm bit and drop them into position so that they rest on the base battens. Arrange them so that the narrow one sits in the middle with the wider ones either side. The base is designed to be removable and, if necessary, renewable. Finish by filling in the countersunk holes in the top capping with wood filler. Varnish inside and out to preserve the wood.

8 Drill holes through the centre of each of the 4 blocks to be used for the feet and screw them, using 3in screws, to each corner of the bottom of the planter.

MAKING A CLASSIC PLANTER

This requires some forethought, so run through the steps first to make sure you understand how it fits together. Start by making two complete sides, then join these with the remaining panels

(*see overleaf*). It is essential that these first sides form a pair. To help achieve this, mark the part of the posts that faces inwards and the base of each post, and always work from the top.

HOW THE PIECES FIT TOGETHER

THE METHOD
There are no difficult joints. Instead, battens and screws are used to fix all the pieces together, as shown in the photographs.

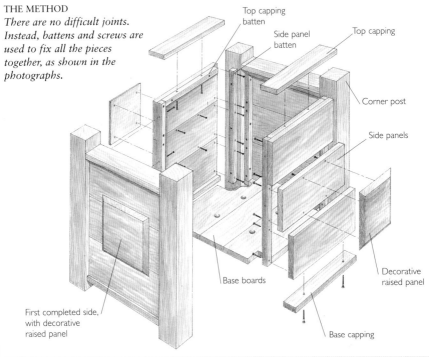

Top capping batten

Side panel batten

Top capping

Corner post

Side panels

Decorative raised panel

Base boards

Base capping

First completed side, with decorative raised panel

YOU NEED:

MATERIALS
- 4 corner posts 54.5×7×7cm
- 8 side panel battens 43×2×2cm
- 12 side panels 32×14.5×2cm
- 4 top capping battens 28×2×2cm
- 4 pieces of top capping 32×7×2cm

- 4 pieces of base capping 32×4.5×2cm
- 2 base boards 38×14.5×2cm
- 1 base board 38×9×2cm
- 4 squares of wood (to make raised panels) 19×19×2.5cm
- 80 size 7, 1¼in (3.2cm) screws
- 20 size 8, 2in (5cm) screws

TOOLS
- Pencil
- Tape measure
- Electric drill
- 4mm drill bit
- Screwdriver
- Set square
- 13mm drill bit, for drainage holes
- Small plane

(All the measurements given here are for finished, planed wood.)

MAKING THE FIRST SIDE

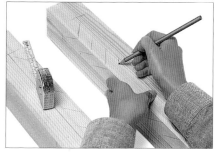

1 On each of a pair of corner posts, make a mark 5.7cm from the top and draw a line down the centre of each inside face. Shade the inner area so you always know which it is.

2 Take 4 side panel battens and drill 3 holes in each, one hole at either end and one in the centre, using the 4mm bit. Always drill onto a spare offcut of wood.

3 Screw 2 battens to each of the pair of corner posts, lining them up with the top mark and just outside your inner shaded area. Always use size 7, 1¼in screws unless otherwise stated. (The side panels will then be screwed to these battens – this forms the basic construction technique.)

4 Hold 3 side panels in turn against the outer edge of the batten, and mark then drill 2 holes per panel in the batten to fix them in place.

5 Lay the 3 side panels in place (propped up by an offcut) and screw them to the batten. Repeat the process to attach them to the other post.

6 Drill 2 holes in a top capping batten and screw it to the top side panel. This will be used to hold the top capping in place (*see overleaf*).

7 **Drill 2 holes** from top to bottom through the top capping batten (avoid the screws that fix it to the side panel) and screw it to the top capping to fix it in place.

8 **Drill 3 holes** in a piece of base capping and screw it (using size 8, 2in screws) into the bottom side panel. It is easiest if you stand the side upside down.

ADDING THE DECORATIVE DETAIL

2 **Shave off** the corner as far as each line, using a small plane.

1 **Mark lines** 12mm from the corner on the top and down the side of the raised panel to show the amount to be chamfered.

3 **Mark the position** of the raised panel on the outside of this first side, making sure that it is in the centre. Mark only the corners. Drill 4 holes within the marked area. (The direction of the grain should match the side panels.)

4 **Screw the panel** in place from the inside. Repeat all these stages to make 2 complete sides.

ASSEMBLING THE PLANTER

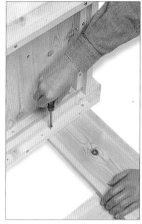

1 Screw 3 side panels to one corner post on each of the finished sides, to form 2 right-angled halves of the planter. Join these together to complete all 4 planter walls.

2 Having drilled and fixed the remaining 2 top capping battens in place (*see p.45, Step 6*), screw the remaining 2 pieces of top capping in position (*above*).

3 Screw the 2 pieces of base capping in place, then the raised panels. Drop the base boards, drilled with drainage holes, into position. Paint or varnish the planter.

DUSKY TONES
The colour of this planter completes a carefully thought-out scheme. The pale slate blue emphasizes the depth of colour of the tulips and purple sage, while the acid green and flame-coloured bracts of the euphorbias in the border provide a brilliant contrast. When they have finished flowering, the tulips can be replaced by mixed annuals in equally interesting colours.

STONE TROUGHS

WORN, WEATHERED AND TURNING GREY-GREEN with patches of lichen, old stone troughs make a perfect setting for plants. Their cost, though, puts them beyond the pocket of most gardeners. By adapting a plastic or polystyrene crate you can make a very plausible substitute for a fraction of the price. You can even make small, substitute "rocks" from hypertufa mixture and place them among the plants, as in the arrangement opposite.

MAKING A HYPERTUFA TROUGH

The traditional alternative to stone is a ceramic sink coated with hypertufa: a mix of cement, sand and peat. But a plastic storage crate is very much cheaper and, once coated, possible to lift without the aid of a fork-lift truck. Polystyrene boxes (*see pp.52–53*) also work well. Peat substitutes can be used in the hypertufa but bark chippings do not bind and make the mix fall apart.

YOU NEED:

MATERIALS
- Plastic crate
- 13mm mesh chicken wire
- 12 wire ties, each 6–8cm long
- Cement
- Sharp sand
- Peat or peat substitute
- Water
- Natural yogurt (or liquid manure)

(Quantities of cement, sand and peat and the length of the chicken wire will all depend on the size of the crate. Proportions are given overleaf.)

TOOLS
- Drill, preferably electric
- 13mm drill bit, for making drainage holes
- Pincers or pliers
- 9-litre bucket or large board, for mixing hypertufa
- Trowel or spade, for mixing
- Rubber gloves
- Paint brush

PREPARING THE CRATE

1 **Make sure** the crate is clean and dry. With foldaway crates (*left*), make sure they are fully open and "clicked" into position. Measure the height and width of each side in preparation for cutting the chicken wire covering (*see overleaf*).

2 **Drill some evenly** spaced drainage holes. You usually need 4–6 depending on the size of the crate. An electric drill, at high speed, is much less likely to crack the plastic than other methods. Drilling onto a spare piece of wood protects your work surface.

◄ AMONG THE ROCKS *A pretty planting of campanulas, auriculas, sedums and saxifrages.*

COVERING WITH WIRE AND HYPERTUFA

1 Cut 4 pieces of chicken wire, using pincers, each large enough to cover the inside and outside of one side. Allow for the pieces to overlap around the corners and tuck under the base by at least 8–10cm.

2 Cover the crate inside and outside with the chicken wire, bending each piece firmly around the corners and tucking it securely around the base. The wire provides the "key" for the hypertufa to adhere to the crate.

3 Thread the wire ties from the outside to the inside of the crate, then back through to tie together the two layers of chicken wire. Use 2–4 ties on each side. This helps prevent a cavity from forming in the hypertufa when it is applied both inside and outside the crate.

4 Mix the hypertufa using, by volume, 1 part cement, 1 part sharp sand and 1–2 parts dry peat or peat substitute. Combine the dry ingredients thoroughly then add sufficient water to make a stiffish mortar. Avoid making the mix too wet or it will not adhere.

PRACTICAL TIPS

• Stand the crate on bricks while applying the hypertufa.
• Leave the hypertufa to dry naturally – the slower the better. You can, if you want, cover it with polythene or damp hessian.
• Avoid working with hypertufa in frosty weather.

5 **Press the hypertufa** in handfuls against the crate walls, inside and out and just under (but not covering) the base. Push it through the chicken wire so that the two layers bond to form a solid wall. Smooth the surface as you go to prevent cracks.

6 **Leave to harden** and, once the hypertufa is dry (usually 2–3 days), paint the surface with yogurt (or liquid manure) to encourage the growth of algae. This helps to give the trough a much more natural look.

CHOOSING APPROPRIATE PLANTS
The plants you choose depend on the size of trough and where you plan to put it. These lavenders suit a large container destined for a sunny spot. Rock plants (see pp.76–77) are the classic choice. They often have small roots and will do well in shallow troughs.

MAKING HYPERTUFA ROCKS

Rocks can greatly enhance alpines in a trough but, to help save natural limestone country and similar areas from unnecessary quarrying, why not try making hypertufa rocks. It is almost inevitable that there will be some mix left over. Simply put some in a plastic bag (*see right*) and shape it into a rock (it may help to have a photograph to copy). Leave to dry slowly. Before the rock hardens completely, you can refine its appearance by adding a few crevices and naturalistic marks.

FAKING A ROCK

TEXTURED CEMENT TROUGH

A polystyrene crate encased in cement mixed with reinforcing fibres produces a trough that is strong, light and has good insulating qualities. A fishmonger or tropical fish stockist is the best source of the crate; reinforcing fibres are used in building ponds and pools and are usually to be found in garden centres rather than DIY stores. It is not necessary to paint the trough, but a splash of colour can make a welcome change from the natural stone look.

YOU NEED:

MATERIALS
- Polystyrene crate
- PVA adhesive
- Cement
- Sharp sand
- Reinforcing fibres
- Water
- Masonry paint

TOOLS
- Drill or knife
- 4–6 corks
- Bricks to stand the crate on
- Large bucket or board, for mixing
- Rubber gloves

MAKING THE TROUGH

1 **Make some** drainage holes in the crate base with a knife or drill and plug with corks so that each cork juts out 2cm beyond the outside of the crate. (The corks will be removed once the cement has set.)

2 **Turn the crate** upside down, keeping it off the ground with a stack of bricks, and coat the outside with a thick layer of PVA adhesive. Leave until the adhesive turns tacky, while you make the cement mixture.

3 **Mix the cement coating** by combining 2 parts cement with 1 part sand, by volume, then adding a handful of the fibres. Fluff them out, work them through the mixture and add enough water to make a stiff mortar.

4 **Press small handfuls** of the mixture all over the outside of the crate, smoothing the surface as you go. The coating needs to be only 1–1.5cm thick. When it has hardened a little, turn the crate the right way up.

6 **Paint the trough,** if desired, once the cement has completely hardened, with masonry or other suitable exterior-quality paint. Remove the corks to create the drainage holes.

5 **Cover the bucket** of cement mix with a damp cloth. Paint the rim and inner edge with PVA, and wait for it to go tacky. Press more mixture around the crate top and down the inside walls to just below planting level.

PRACTICAL HINTS

• If you prefer, you can give the trough a smooth finish by burning off the ends of the fibres before painting.

• Because this type of reinforcing fibre makes the cement mixture exceptionally strong, the coating around the crate can be made quite thin (just over 1cm) without any danger of the trough cracking.

• If using a crate from the fishmonger, after rinsing it you will probably need to allow time for the fish smell to disappear.

CHOOSING PLANTS

Rock plants such as small campanulas, achilleas and sedums are ideal for shallow troughs. The diascias here, unfortunately, are not reliably hardy and may have to be renewed the following season. For this kind of planting, it is essential to use a free-draining compost (see p.55).

Acaena
saccaticupula
'Blue Haze'

Campanula
carpatica 'Isabel'

Thymus vulgaris
'Silver Posie'

Campanula
carpatica 'Jewel'

Scutellaria
indica var.
parvifolia

Diascia
'Lilac Belle'

Achillea × lewisii
'King Edward'

Sedum
spathulifolium
'Cape Blanco'

Thymus
'Doone
Valley'

PLANTING AND ROUTINE CARE

CARING FOR PLANTS IN POTS

UNLIKE PLANTS IN THE OPEN GROUND, container plants are dependent on watering and feeding. Evergreens may even need watering in winter, when the drying effect of wind can be particularly damaging. Regular watering tends to compact soil, so always use one of the special potting composts available (*see opposite*), which drain freely and hold sufficient air, moisture and nutrients to sustain plant growth. Stand containers on wedges or feet to aid drainage.

PREPARING FOR PLANTING

Make sure that there are adequate drainage holes in the base of containers; if using an improvised or home-made container, you may need to drill some. It is essential that plant roots never become waterlogged. Cover the pot base with crocks or other drainage material to prevent loss of compost without impeding drainage. It is also a good idea to use pot feet or wedges to raise the container slightly so that water can drain freely, especially in winter. As a precaution against compost drying out for short periods, mix in water-retentive crystals, which swell up with moisture then later release it. When planting in large containers, more surface area of compost is exposed to sunlight so it is a good idea to mulch with pebbles or gravel to conserve moisture.

GRAVEL

Crystals swell
on contact
with water

POLYSTYRENE

ADDING CROCKS
Broken pieces of terracotta, or "crocks", are the most traditional material for covering the base of a container, but gravel, pebbles or polystyrene pieces make a good alternative.

USING WATER-RETENTIVE CRYSTALS
Mix water-retentive crystals thoroughly into the compost before planting to help plants through short spells of dryness. Never add more than the recommended amount.

WHICH COMPOST TO CHOOSE

Do not be tempted to use garden soil for container planting, because of the danger of introducing pests, worms, weed seeds and even diseases. Using a formulated potting compost eliminates all these risks. Chosen carefully for the particular planting you have in mind (for instance, there are composts designed specially for trees and shrubs), it will include exactly the right balance of nutrients and adequate drainage material to encourage healthy plant growth over a period of time. Loam-based composts contain prepared, sterilized soil of ideal texture and composition, and are heavy, often making pots more stable. Peat- or peat substitute-based composts are light but, if they dry out, can be difficult to re-wet.

A great advantage of container growing is that you can cater to the likes and dislikes of particular plants. Favourite plants that do not grow well in your garden's soil can be encouraged to thrive in containers filled with compost tailor-made to meet their requirements.

TYPES OF COMPOST

JOHN INNES (LOAM-BASED)

John Innes composts are a series of specially formulated loam-based composts. No. 3 is the one to use for long-term planting; loam holds nutrients for a considerable time. It is suitable for trees and shrubs, such as *Fatsia japonica* (*right*), and also for perennials.

GENERAL PURPOSE (SOILLESS)

Peat- or peat substitute-based multi-purpose composts are ideal for flowering annuals, such as *Tagetes* (*right*), and plants that are used in displays which last only for a few months. These composts are light and easy to handle, but dry out easily and need regular checking.

ERICACEOUS (LIME-FREE)

Plants that cannot tolerate lime such as rhododendrons, pieris and some species of *Erica*, need acidic or "ericaceous" compost. Lime also affects flower colour in plants such as hydrangeas (*right*). Use ericaceous compost if blue-flowered cultivars are to stay blue.

ALPINE (FREE-DRAINING)

Alpine compost includes plenty of coarse grit to give the extra drainage needed by rock plants, such as *Androsace* (*right*). You can also mix your own by adding grit to a loam-based compost. A surface dressing of coarse grit helps to prevent stem-rot due to winter wet.

PLANTING IN CONTAINERS

Small trees, shrubs and perennials that will live in containers long-term need a compost that will satisfy their nutritional demands over an extended period. They also require good-sized containers, large enough for their roots to develop properly and heavy enough to stay upright in wind. Annuals and small bulbs are useful for adding seasonal colour under permanent plantings.

PLANTING INDIVIDUAL SHRUBS

When planting a single specimen shrub for immediate impact, it is best to choose a plant that is 2–3 years old and container-grown in a large pot. The new container must be sturdy and large enough to allow a minimum of 5–8cm of new compost under the shrub's root ball and around its sides. There must also be sufficient depth for a layer of drainage material to be added to the base of the container. Before planting, it is important to water the shrub thoroughly and allow it to drain.

1 Fill the container loosely with some compost. Use the shrub's old pot as a guide to check that the plant will sit at the correct depth.

2 Tease out some fine roots gently around the sides and base of the root ball. Lower the shrub into the container. Firm the plant in.

3 Add any extra compost that is needed, making sure you leave space at the top of the pot for watering. Water in thoroughly.

UNDERPLANTING A SHRUB

Some fast-growing shrubs (like the pieris, right) require large containers such as half-barrels to accommodate their roots and provide a visual balance to their ultimate size. To give the planting additional interest while the shrub is small, use colourful annuals which, with their shallow roots, will not compete for food or space. Winter-flowering pansies make an excellent choice for a site that catches the sun at that time of year. They will be happy in the ericaceous compost used to suit the pieris. In summer, there is a wider range of bedding plants to choose from.

The barrel must be waterproofed inside and out with varnish

Barrel must have drainage holes

MAKING THE MOST OF BULBS

Many bulbs, such as daffodils, are resilient enough to be planted in 3–4 tiers in a large pot. Concentrating a number of bulbs in a small area gives a generous display. Ivy will cascade over the edges of the pot and winter-flowering pansies produce a second flush just as daffodils come into bloom.

Dense planting of daffodils provides masses of flowers

Winter-flowering pansies require some sun to bloom

Ivy planted at edge

Bulbs are planted in alternate tiers

Crocks

1 **Cross-section** shows a drainage layer, 3 layers of bulbs in general-purpose compost and surface planting.

2 **Winter interest** is maintained by variegated ivy and pansies. Deadheading encourages new blooms.

3 **In spring** the display is at its best, with the daffodils blooming above a carpet of ivy and pansies.

MIXED PLANTINGS

Spring-planted perennials will make splendid container displays through summer, but you may need to divide and replant them for the following season, particularly if grouping more than one plant in a pot. Site the tallest plants in the centre of the display and let trailing types spill over the edges.

Heuchera micrantha 'Palace Purple'

Penstemon 'Rich Ruby'

Artemisia 'Powis Castle'

◀ PLANTING TIME
Group the plants while still in their pots to decide on the best arrangement. Then plant, firm in and water well.

▶ IN FULL GLORY
This display uses plants with good contrasts in foliage colour and forms. Most perennials tolerate trimming if they start swamping their neighbours.

Geranium sanguineum var. *striatum*

ROUTINE CARE

Plants in containers need regular attention. Do not rely on rainfall to keep them watered, except perhaps in winter. Compost needs to be kept moist but not soggy; use pot feet or wedges to raise containers off the ground and allow water to drain freely. Fast-acting liquid feeds are easy to use. Choose those high in nitrogen for foliage plants and high-potash formulations for flowers.

WATERING AND FEEDING

In summer try to water at the start or end of the day when less will be lost through evaporation. Hot sun on wet leaves causes them to scorch. A slow-release fertilizer plug pushed into compost supplies nutrients gradually but for maximum flowers give plants a fortnightly boost of tomato feed.

SLOW-RELEASE FERTILIZER PLUGS

Direct the water to the compost; if sprinkled onto leaves it will run straight off

EFFECTIVE WATERING
Soak the compost directly or fill a saucer or tray beneath so that the plant drinks it up.

RENEWING THE DISPLAY

Remove bedding plants from containers when they finish flowering, disturbing those that remain as little as possible. To maintain the display, replace them with plants that have a later flowering season or striking foliage. You can also add bulbs to continue interest over a longer period.

DEADHEADING
Deadheading is vital to encourage plants to continue flowering. Pinch off dead blooms between your thumb and forefinger.

Pick off any dead leaves regularly

Evergreen foliage plants such as ivy give year-round interest

1 Remove plants that have finished flowering, taking care not to damage the roots of remaining plants. Continue deadheading to encourage more flowers.

2 Add fresh potting compost and fill the gaps with new plants or bulbs that will continue the display. Firm gently and water thoroughly to help the new plants to establish.

REPLENISHING COMPOST

Most shrubs, once fully grown, can stay in the same pot for several years if nourished by a top-dressing of fresh potting compost applied each spring. To ensure good plant growth, mix in fertilizer with the compost.

Compost loses its nutrients in time

TOP-DRESSING
Scrape off about 5cm of compost. Replace this top layer with fresh compost mixed with a slow-release fertilizer; then water thoroughly.

WINTER SHELTER

Many lovely container plants will not survive winter cold. Any with foliage that dies down (e.g. agapanthus) can be put in a shed or garage. Others need protection and light.

✱✱✱ Even fully hardy plants are vulnerable in pots. In very cold areas, or if a plant is described as "borderline hardy", move to the most sheltered side of the house, or bury to the rim in a border and dry-mulch with straw.

✱✱ Frost hardy plants need to be moved into a cold frame or greenhouse. Some survive outside if pots are swathed in hessian or bubble-wrap to insulate roots. Use this to wrap leaves, too, of phormiums and yuccas.

✱ Half-hardy plants should be put in an unheated greenhouse or conservatory.

Tender plants (e.g. citrus) need to be moved into a heated greenhouse or conservatory.

Protect your back – use a trolley or board fitted with castors to move large containers.

REPOTTING AN OVERGROWN PLANT

When a plant outgrows its container, it will lose vigour and start showing signs of poor health such as yellowing leaves. To check whether it needs repotting, remove the plant carefully from its container and examine the roots. If they are crowded, you need to repot the plant into a larger container. Select one that is one or two sizes larger. Make sure that it is clean in order to avoid introducing diseases.

1 Ease the plant gently from its pot by a combination of tapping the rim and pulling gently on the base of the stems.

2 Tease out roots that have become very congested and cut back thick roots by about a third. Leave the thin fibrous roots intact.

3 Put crocks and fresh compost in the new pot and lower in the plant. Add compost around the edges and firm in. Add support for climbers (*here ivy*) and tie in stems (*see inset*). Water well.

TRAINING STANDARDS

S TANDARD PLANTS IN POTS can bring formal elegance to courtyards, patios and doorways. Standards that are destined for a prominent position deserve a handsome but sturdy container. Choose a size and style that will balance the height and width of the plant. When fully grown, most standards need regular trimming to keep them in shape and frequent feeding in the growing season.

TRAINING A STANDARD FUCHSIA

Shrubby plants such as fuchsias grow quickly and produce soft shoots that can be "pinch-pruned" to make bushy heads. No equipment is needed; sideshoots and then shoot tips, once the head starts to form, are simply pinched out between finger and thumb. Start with a young plant about 15cm high. It takes 6 months to achieve a 45cm standard and 18 months to grow a full 100cm-high standard, so plants that are not hardy will need shelter in winter.

OTHER SUITABLE PLANTS

Argyranthemum frutescens
Cascade chrysanthemums
Helichrysum petiolare
Heliotropium arborescens (Heliotrope)
Lantana camara
Solenostemon scutellaroides (Coleus)

FLOWERS GALORE
*Choose a vigorous,
free-flowering fuchsia
(e.g. 'White Ann').
Remove old leaves
from the main
stem that do not
naturally fall.*

1 **Pinch out** any sideshoots as they appear in the leaf angles. Insert a cane and tie in the stem to keep it straight.

2 **Keep removing** sideshoots (never the tip) to produce a tall, straight stem. Transfer to a bigger pot with a taller cane.

3 **When the stem** is 3 sets of leaves taller than you want the clear trunk of the standard to be, pinch out the growing tip.

4 **Pinch out** the tips of the sideshoots at the top of the stem to make them branch further. Repeat until a round head is formed.

TRAINING STANDARD TREES

Many trees, such as citrus and bays, can be bought as standards but are expensive. If you have a little patience, they are not particularly difficult to train yourself, though it takes several years. Start with a healthy young plant with an upright main stem that will naturally lend itself to training. Tie this in to a cane just taller than you want the clear trunk to be. You will need secateurs when stems turn woody.

TREES AND SHRUBS FOR STANDARDS

Brugmansia (Angels' trumpets)
Citrus trees: Calamondin
(× *Citrofortunella microcarpa*),
a mandarin-kumquat hybrid;
Citrus × *meyeri* 'Meyer';
C. *aurantium* (Seville orange)

Laurus nobilis (Bay)
Pittosporum
Nerium oleander
Syringa meyeri
Viburnum tinus

Prune the main stem back to a strong bud just below the top of the cane

Prune shoots by 3–5 leaves. As more shoots develop, continue pruning in the same way to form a well-shaped head

Cane makes stem grow straight

Leaves on shortened sideshoots feed and thicken the trunk

Select 4 strong, well-spaced framework shoots from which to develop the head

Remove all subsequent shoots from the main stem. Leaves on it will be shed naturally

Keep tip-pruning new shoots to make the head bushier

Calamondin enjoys an ericaceous compost

1 Tie in the main stem; tip-prune it once it reaches the desired height. Shorten side-shoots by a third in their first year; remove the year after.

2 Let 4 strong shoots develop to form the head. Shorten them to make them branch, then shorten their sideshoots in turn.

A MATURE TREE
The cane and ties can be removed as soon as the stem becomes woody and the plant is well established.

CREATING INTERESTING SHAPES

SMALL-LEAVED IVIES ARE EASILY TURNED into "topiary" using a wire shape or, with time, you can make a masterpiece in box or yew using more traditional techniques. Some plants can be pinch-pruned, enabling you to create pillars and cones, even fans, around a simple frame of canes. Climbers can be trained over hazel tripods, wire obelisks or willow balloons.

TRAINED AND CLIPPED TOPIARY

Some of the simplest but most effective topiary is created by letting ivy grow around a wire frame. Shoots will need occasional tying in or trimming off. You can buy purpose-made animal or geometric wire shapes or make your own. Try moulding chicken wire into three-dimensional creatures (*see p.13*). Use a frame, too, for conventional topiary in box or yew. It makes clipping very much easier.

▶ IVY SEA HORSE
Plastic-coated wire has been bent into a sea horse shape. Wire zig-zagged across the centre of the shape strengthens it and gives extra support for the ivy to cling to.

PLANTS FOR TOPIARY

***Buxus sempervirens* 'Suffruticosa'** ♀ Box
***Hedera helix* 'Bill Archer'** Ivy with tiny leaves
***Hedera helix* 'Goldheart'** (syn. 'Oro di Bogliasco') Gold-variegated ivy
Taxus baccata ♀ Yew

USING A TOPIARY FRAME

1 **Place the frame** over the plant (*here yew*), securing it into the compost. Trim the tips of all the shoots to encourage the plant to make bushy growth that will fill out the frame.

2 **Trim shoots** when they start growing beyond the edge of the frame, using the frame as a guide for cutting. Secateurs are often better than shears for clipping small, detailed shapes.

3 **Foliage hides** the frame when the topiary is mature. It will need regular trimming to keep a neat outline, generally at least 3–4 times a year depending on the intricacy of the shape.

TRAINING A HELICHRYSUM CONE

With frequent pinch-pruning (*see p.60*), spreading plants such as *Helichrysum petiolare* can be trained to make a dense, leafy cone, ideal for adding height to a display. Helichrysums grow fast and should reach the top of a metre-high cane wigwam in one season. In cold areas, protect under glass in winter for the following season.

Pinch sideshoots to a leaf or bud so that none extends beyond the width of the pot

Use soft twine to tie the leading, upright stems to the canes that will form the wigwam

FLORAL EFFECT

A helichrysum is grown for foliage effect but, with plants such as fuchsias and ivy-leaved pelargoniums, once you stop pinch-pruning flowerbuds will form and the cone will be covered with flowers.

1 Plant 3 young plants in a pot. Insert 3 canes, the height of the cone. Tie in the leading, upright shoots. Pinch all sideshoots to a bud or leaf in line with the edge of the pot.

Pinch the sideshoots once a week to develop a conical shape and make the plants bushy (this side has still to be pinched)

Pinch out the tips of the leading stems once they reach the top

Pinch to keep a smooth line up the side of the cone

2 Tie the canes to form a wigwam. Keep tying in the leading shoots and pinching sideshoots to develop a dense, well-shaped cone. Put into a sturdy container for display.

FINISHED CONE
This cone has been left to grow out to give an informal look, but it could also be trimmed with shears to create a clean-cut topiary effect.

GOOD PLANTS FOR CONTAINERS

This selection of plants is arranged according to the type of container and style of display that suits them best, but there are no hard and fast rules and planting arrangements will always need to suit individual requirements.

▨ *Prefers full sun* ▨ *Prefers partial shade* ▧ *Tolerates full shade* CH, CS *Approximate container height and spread* ✻✻✻ *Fully hardy* ✻✻ *Frost hardy* ✻ *Half-hardy* ♀*RHS Award of Garden Merit*

RECOMMENDED LARGE PLANTS

MANY OF THE FOLLOWING TREES, shrubs and climbers make good specimen plants for large containers. Pots must be stable and compost will need revitalizing regularly. Some of the most useful architectural plants are not fully hardy and in cold areas will require protection in winter (*see p.59*).

Abutilon pictum 'Thomsonii'
Shrub with orange bell flowers in summer and mottled maple-shaped leaves. Requires a sheltered sunny site; protect in winter in a greenhouse or conservatory. The abutilon 'Souvenir de Bonn' ♀ has cream-margined leaves.
▨ CH 1.2–2m CS 1m ✻

Acer palmatum (Japanese maple)
Small tree good for adding a Japanese flavour, especially in a glazed pot. Deciduous, deeply cut leaves often show brilliant autumn colour. *A. palmatum* 'Dissectum Atropurpureum' (*see p.17*) has almost feathery leaves. Avoid exposed sites where wind may scorch leaves.
▧ CH 1.2m CS 1.5–2m ✻✻✻

Aralia elata ♀
Architectural tree for light shade. Deciduous, divided leaves are arranged in elegant tiers; the leaves are edged cream in 'Variegata'.
▨ CH 3m CS 2m ✻✻✻

BRUGMANSIA AUREA

Brugmansia (Angels' trumpets, Datura)
Huge trumpets usually have superb fragrance. Those of *B. aurea* smell best in evening. Other species can have white or pink trumpets. Flowers are produced most freely with the restriction of a container. Evergreen, but needs some warmth in winter. Toxic.
▨ CH 2m CS 1–2m Min 7°C

Buxus sempervirens (Common box)
Ideal for container topiary (*see pp.13, 62*). Slow-growing shrub with dense stems of small evergreen leaves that can be clipped to geometric or animal shapes. You can buy wire frames that act as a guide for clipping.
▨ CH to 2.5m CS to 1m ✻✻✻

CONVOLVULUS CNEORUM

Camellia japonica

Good shrub in a container against a west or sheltered north wall where early spring flowers are less likely to be browned by frost. Many good cultivars with single or double flowers in red, pink or white. Use ericaceous compost.
CH 2m CS 1m ✿✿✿

Citrus

Highly decorative and, in a warm climate, productive small trees or shrubs. Sweet-smelling white flowers are followed by fruit. *C.* × *meyeri* 'Meyer' is a compact hybrid lemon. × *Citrofortunella microcarpa*, the calamondin, has small decorative fruit that can be crystallized. In cold areas plants need the warmth of a conservatory or greenhouse in winter.
CH to 2m CS to 1.5m
Min 3–5°C

Convolvulus cneorum ♀

Sun-loving shrub with silvery leaves and white flowers that will tumble over the sides of a pot from late spring to mid-summer. Appreciates some winter protection from cold winds and requires good drainage. It can be tricky.
CH 45cm CS 60cm ✿✿

Cordyline australis ♀

Palm-like tree that creates a highly sculptural effect (*see p.10*). Some cultivars have striped or plum-coloured leaves. Excellent in urban settings. Tolerates light shade but needs the winter protection of a greenhouse or conservatory in cold areas.
CH 2–3m CS 1–1.2m ✿

Cupressus torulosa 'Cashmeriana' ♀

Extremely elegant conifer with sprays of pendulous blue leaves. A large tree when planted in the ground but a container keeps it to a manageable size. Move into a greenhouse or conservatory in cold areas in winter.
CH 3m CS 1.5m ✿

Cycas revoluta ♀

Architectural, exotic-looking palm-like plant, with shaggy trunk and shuttlecock of fringed leathery leaves. Native of Japan; in cold areas it needs winter warmth in a

× FATSHEDERA LIZEI

FATSIA JAPONICA

greenhouse or conservatory.
CH 1–2m CS 1–2m
Min 7–10°C

Eriobotrya japonica

(Loquat) ♀
Striking evergreen shrub or small tree with large, veined, leathery leaves. In a sheltered site, fragrant white autumn flowers are followed in spring by orange edible fruit. Preferably place against a sheltered sunny wall.
CH 2–3m CS 2–3m ✿✿

× Fatshedera lizei ♀

Evergreen shrub useful for training up a vertical support. Large ivy-like leaves and greenish-white flowers in autumn. Particularly tolerant of poor conditions such as exposure, pollution, shade.
CH to 2m CS 1m ✿✿

Fatsia japonica ♀

Spreading, architectural shrub for a shaded, sheltered courtyard. Evergreen, with large, many-lobed, glossy leaves. Creamy-white flowers in autumn are followed by black berries.
CH 1.5m CS 1m–1.2m ✿✿

HYDRANGEA MACROPHYLLA 'BLUE WAVE'

Hydrangea macrophylla

Hydrangeas look particularly good in half-barrels or wooden planters. Blue flowers are produced only in acidic soil, so using ericaceous compost in pots enables you to grow blue cultivars in alkaline areas. Those known as "lacecaps", like 'Blue Wave' (*above*), have flowerheads composed of sterile and fertile flowers. The "mopheads" have rounded heads of only sterile flowers. Prune established plants in spring, cutting back one in four old flowering stems to the base. Trim off other old flower-heads to the next leaf bud.
✿ ▣ CH 1m CS 1.8m ✳✳✳

Ilex crenata

(Box-leaved holly)
Neat holly with glossy, oval, dark green leaves. Sometimes produces white or yellow fruit from inconspicuous flowers. Makes a useful year-round shrub. 'Convexa' ♀ is broader and denser in habit and produces masses of shiny black fruits.
✿ CH 2m CS 1m ✳✳✳

Lantana

Evergreen shrub grown for its vivid flowers, sometimes bicolored, ranging from white to yellow and salmon-pink to red or purple, in late summer and autumn. Needs warmth in winter. Can be grown as a standard (*see p.60*).
✿ CH 1m CS 1m Min 10°C

Laurus nobilis (Bay laurel) ♀

Handsome evergreen shrub or small tree which doubles as a culinary herb. In spring, clusters of greenish-yellow flowers are produced, followed by black berries on female plants only. It enjoys the warmth of a sunny wall. Adapts well to clipping and can be grown as a standard (*see pp.22, 61*).
✿ CH 2–3m CS 1–2m ✳✳

Lavandula (Lavender)

Aromatic, easy to grow and attracts butterflies and bees. *L. angustifolia* can have pink or white flowers as well as the more usual blue-purple. 'Hidcote' ♀ is compact with dense purple flower spikes. *L. stoechas* (*see p.9*) is more tender and may need winter protection. All need free-draining compost. Keep lavenders in shape by cutting back in spring, always leaving some green growth.
✿ CH 60cm CS 1m ✳✳✳

LANTANA 'TANGERINE'

MYRTUS COMMUNIS

Myrtus communis ♀

(Common myrtle)
Small aromatic shrub that will scent a sitting area. Delightful fragrant ivory flowers stand out against evergreen leaves in late summer. Place out of cold winds in winter. *M. communis* subsp. *tarentina* ♀ has smaller leaves and makes a more rounded shape.
✿ CH 1m CS 1m ✳✳

Nerium oleander (Oleander)

A Mediterranean reminder for city gardens. In summer, clusters of pink, red or white flowers cover this narrow-leaved shrub or small tree (*see p.61*). In cold areas, protect in a conservatory or greenhouse in winter. Toxic.
✿ CH 2m CS 1–1.5m Min 2–5°C

Phormium tenax ♀

(New Zealand flax)
Striking foliage plant with upright sword-like leaves. Tall stems bear heads of dull red flowers in summer. Some phormiums have bronze or interestingly striped foliage. 'Dazzler' is small with bronze leaves streaked with red,

orange and pink; those of 'Variegatum' ♀ have creamy-yellow margins. Move to a sheltered spot for winter in cold areas and insulate the pot with a layer of bubble-wrap or hessian. You can also wrap the leaves in a sheath of protective material.
◨ CH to 2m CS to 1m ✽✽

Rosa (Rose)
Choose dwarf cluster-flowered or miniature bush forms, often described as "patio roses", for growing in containers and allow plenty of depth for their long roots. Anna Ford ♀ has a compact habit and orange-red flowers. It has little scent. Sweet Magic ♀ has golden orange flower with a delicate scent. Mid-pink 'Stacey Sue' ♀ is worth trying. All bloom freely through the summer.
◨ CH to 45cm CS to 40cm ✽✽✽

Rosmarinus officinalis
(Rosemary)
Aromatic shrub for a sunny site. Ideally, put in a sheltered spot near the kitchen door or barbecue – the needle-like leaves are excellent for flavouring grilled food. Blue flowers cover the stems from spring to early summer. 'Prostratus' ♀ looks good trailing over the sides of a container but is more tender. Plants must have free-draining compost and benefit from winter protection.
◨ CH to 1m CS 1m ✽✽

Salix caprea 'Kilmarnock' ♀
(Kilmarnock willow)
Small weeping tree (*see p.16*) whose shape gives all-year interest. Bare branches in spring are studded with furry catkins. A subtly coloured planter and ring of snowdrops complete the picture.
◨ CH 1.5–2m CS 2m ✽✽✽

Viburnum tinus
(Laurustinus)
A shade-tolerant and reliable shrub for a container; it can also be grown as a standard (*see p.61*). The flat heads of white flowers against evergreen leaves look good in winter. Underplant with annual bedding for summer colour.
◨◨ CH 1.2m CS 1.2m ✽✽✽

Yucca
Spiky evergreen for a sunny corner (*see p.27*). Match its exotic looks with a handsome container. Tall spikes of white bells rise from the centre in late summer. *Y. filamentosa* ♀ is quite small and is hardy. *Y. gloriosa* ♀ and yellow-striped 'Variegata' ♀ are tall and slightly tender; they can be protected in the same way as a phormium (*see left*). Use free-draining compost.
◨ CH to 1.5m CS to 1m ✽✽✽

SOME CLIMBERS FOR CONTAINERS

These climbers give colour and height. For support, insert a wigwam of canes or use one of the attractive purpose-made frames of trellis or hazel.

Ipomoea tricolor 'Heavenly Blue' ♀
(Morning glory)
Succession of glorious azure trumpets open each morning in a sunny spot. Fast-growing; best treated as an annual and can be raised from seed on an indoor windowsill. Put several plants in one large pot.
◨ CH 3m Min 7°C

Lathyrus odoratus
(Sweet pea)
Provides delicious scent in summer and early autumn. Huge range of colours available; regular picking prolongs flowering. An annual, but you can buy pots of seedlings or raise your own from seed. The Bijou Group is smaller, needing less support, but has less scent.
◨ CH to 2m ✽✽✽

Plumbago auriculata ♀
Evergreen climbing shrub with sky-blue flowers from summer to late autumn as long as roots are not kept too

wet. It needs protection in winter in cold areas. Good in conservatories.
◨ CH 3m CS 1–3m ✽

LATHYRUS 'NOEL SUTTON'

PLANTS FOR GROUPED CONTAINERS

SOME OF THE MOST EFFECTIVE displays combine separate pots each containing a different type of plant. Individual needs, such as special compost or winter protection, can be catered for and plants easily added or removed without disturbing roots. The following work well in this kind of scheme.

FUCHSIA 'LADY THUMB'

Agapanthus
Round heads of blue or white flowers on tall stems in mid–late summer (*see p.40*). Plants can be moved into position when about to flower. Many cultivars are fairly hardy but in cold areas put into a shed or cold frame for winter or sink the pot into the ground.
🔲 CH to 1m CS to 60cm ✿✿

Chrysanthemum
Rubellum chrysanthemums make good late summer and early autumn pot plants, in a variety of colours with yellow centres to the flowers. They form bushy plants with slightly silvery foliage.
🔲 CH 60cm CS to 60cm ✿✿✿

Eucomis bicolor
Has striking spikes of green flowers in late summer (*see p.19*). A bulbous perennial

that needs the protection of a shed or cold frame in winter.
🔲 CH to 60cm CS to 30cm ✿✿

Fuchsia
Upright fuchsias add height when grown as standards (*see p.60*), while trailing types are excellent in a tall pot or windowbox (*see p.30*). Wide choice, with single or double flowers in combinations of red, white, pink and purple produced all summer. Most need unheated winter protection but plantlets are readily available in spring.
🔳 CH to 60cm (as a bush) CS to 60cm ✿✿

Galtonia candicans
Late summer bulb with white tubular flowers (*see p.40*). Protect pots or lift bulbs for winter in cold climates.
🔲 CH 1–1.2m CS 10cm ✿✿✿

Helianthus annuus
Sunflowers (*see p.7*) in pots can be moved around so that they face you, not the sun. Choose short-growing types such as the 'Music Box' range with flowers from creamy-yellow to dark red. Annual; easy to raise from seed.
🔲 CH 45cm CS 45cm ✿✿✿

Lilium (Lily)
Lilies give colour, many have wonderful fragrance and, grown in their own pot, can be moved at their peak into prime position. Use deep pots and plant bulbs at 2–3 times their depth. The majority prefer ericaceous compost but check individual species and hybrids. Short-growing lilies are easier than tall types, which need staking. Feed occasionally with high-potash fertilizer. There is a huge

INTERESTING SUCCULENTS

With their rosettes of fleshy leaves, succulents have an interesting textural quality, especially if planted in a terracotta pot. They need gritty, free-draining compost.

Aeonium arboreum ♀
One of the taller succulents. The leaves of 'Zwartkop' are almost black (*see p.8*). Perennial, but overwinter in

a conservatory or heated greenhouse.
🔲 CH 60cm CS 1m
Min 10°C

Echeveria elegans ♀
Rosettes of silver-blue leaves are sometimes edged red. Best grown as an annual. Useful for shallow pots.
🔲 CH 5cm CS 50cm
Min 7°C

LILIUM 'STAR GAZER'

range to choose from, for sun or part shade. For mid-summer fragrance, try white *L. regale*; it varies in height. The following Asiatic hybrids lack scent but are easy to grow: 'Connecticut King', with rich yellow, long-lasting flowers; 'Enchantment', orange and short-growing; scarlet 'Fire King'; 'Mont Blanc', short-growing with bowl-shaped white flowers. Pinkish-red, unscented 'Star Gazer' also flowers at this time; it is quite tall. Later in summer come *L. auratum* ♥ with white flowers banded gold and tall *L. speciosum* ♥ with white flowers spotted crimson; both are fragrant but more tricky. ▨▨ CH to 1.2m ✻✻✻

Tulipa (Tulip)
Extensive range to choose from for spring–early summer flowers (*see pp.11, 19*). Some short-stemmed types such as scarlet 'Fusilier' and pink and cream 'Heart's Delight' are good for windowsills. After flowering, lift and replant bulbs in the garden if possible. ▨ CH to 60cm ✻✻✻

GOOD FOLIAGE PLANTS

Asplenium scolopendrium
(Hart's tongue fern)
Glossy evergreen fronds brighten a shady corner. Some kinds have curious, crested, wavy-edged fronds. ▨▨ CH 45–70cm CS 60cm ✻✻✻

Chionochloa conspicua
(Plumed tussock grass)
Ornamental grass with tussocks of red-brown leaves that throw up elegant plumes of creamy flowerheads in mid–late summer. Makes an excellent container specimen in 2–3 years. Protect from winter wet. ▨ CH 1.2m CS 1m ✻✻

Hakonechloa macra 'Aureola'
Perennial grass that makes shaggy mounds of yellow leaves, flushed red in autumn – a good contrast with broad- or large-leaved plants. ▨ CH 35cm CS 40cm ✻✻✻

Heuchera micrantha 'Palace Purple' ♥
Large, almost metallic, purple leaves (*see p.15*) look handsome in a pot. Sprays of tiny white flowers appear in summer. ▨ CH to 45cm CS 45cm ✻✻✻

Hosta (Plantain lily)
Grown for their bold foliage, the many hostas

on offer are excellent for containers in shade (*see p.11*). Leaf sizes can vary greatly. Colour varies too; some leaves are variegated cream or yellow, others are nearly blue. Pale bell-shaped flowers are a late summer bonus. In pots hostas tend to be less vulnerable to slug damage. ▨ CH to 60cm CS to 60cm ✻✻✻*IUM* . 'BELLINGHAM

Polystichum setiferum
(Soft shield fern)
Evergreen fern with fronds arranged in a shuttlecock. Delicate yet architectural; invaluable for winter interest. ▨ CH 45cm CS 45cm ✻✻✻

Sasa palmata f. *nebulosa* ♥
Containers keep spreading bamboos within bounds. This one has handsome, broad leaves. Shelter it from winter wind to prevent them from browning. Divide plant once it fills its pot. ▨ CH 1.8m CS indefinite ✻✻✻

POLYSTICHUM SETIFERUM

MIXED DISPLAYS

Combining a range of plants in one large container produces eye-catching results but needs planning – all must enjoy the same conditions. They will also need careful management for a sustained display. On the other hand, compost in large containers is slower to dry out so less water may be needed.

Argyranthemum (Marguerite)
A bright summer plant for large mixed tubs. White, golden-eyed daisies appear continuously all summer. In cold areas, overwinter in a greenhouse or conservatory, or buy new plants each year. There are many named argyranthemums including: 'Jamaica Primrose' ♀, with yellow flowers; 'Mary Wootton', with pink flowers fading white; 'Vancouver' ♀, with pink flowers fading buff. Evergreen, and can be trained as standards (*see p.60*).
▣ CH to 70cm CS to 70cm ✳

Ballota pseudodictamnus ♀
Forms attractive mounds of woolly grey-green leaves with whorls of pinkish-white flowers in spring and early summer. Needs good drainage.
▣ CH 45cm CS 45cm ✳✳✳

ARGYRANTHEMUM FRUTESCENS

Begonia semperflorens
Compact plants, sometimes with bronze leaves, are covered in small red, pink or white flowers throughout summer. Will flower in shade. The Cocktail Series ♀ stands up well to wet weather. Best treated as an annual; do not put out young plants until all danger of frost has passed.
▣ CH 20–30cm CS 30cm Min 13°C

Celosia argentea
(Cockscomb)
Plumes of bright feather-like flowers, often red or gold, stand well above the pale green leaves. The Fairy Fountains range includes pink, salmon and pale yellow. Best treated as an annual.
▣ CH 40cm CS 35cm ✳

Diascia
Long-flowering perennials with several good choices for pots. Flowers range from pink to apricot to lilac. Not reliably hardy but more likely to survive winter if given good drainage. *D. rigescens* ♀ has pink flowers on tall dense spikes and will trail and soften the edges of a container. 'Ruby Field' has deep pink, more open flower spikes. 'Lilac Belle' (*see p.53*) is good among silver-leaved plants such as ballota.
▣ CH 15–30cm CS to 50cm ✳✳

GERBERA JAMESONII

Gerbera jamesonii
Vivid scarlet flowers appear from late spring to late summer. Selections such as the Pandora Series offer a wider colour range including cream, apricot and lavender. Though perennial, treat as an annual in cold climates.
▣ CH 30–45cm CS 60cm Min 5°C

Helichrysum petiolare ♀
Trailing stems of grey woolly leaves are excellent in any mixed plantings in window-boxes and pots of all sizes. Can also be trained up canes to form a dense pillar of foliage (*see p.63*). 'Limelight' has lime-green leaves. Loves baking in strong sun. Cut back shoots threatening to overwhelm other plants. Best treated as an annual.
▣ CH to 30cm CS 1m ✳

Heliotropium arborescens
(Heliotrope, Cherry pie)
Has wonderfully fragrant violet-blue flowers in summer. Place near a sitting area or grow in a windowbox where the scent will also waft into indoor rooms. Usually treated as an annual.
◨ CH 45cm CS 30–45cm ✳

Hyacinthus orientalis
(Hyacinth)
Flower spikes of pink, white, pale to deep blue, yellow or orange add fragrance and colour in early spring to evergreen displays. After flowering, bulbs can be planted out in the garden.
◨◧ CH 20–30cm CS 8cm ✳✳✳

Impatiens walleriana
(Busy lizzie)
Flowers throughout summer even in shade; foliage can vary from green to bronze. Flowers may be double or single, in many colours. The Tempo Series range includes violet, lavender, orange, pink and red with several bicolours and picotees. Treat as an annual and do not be tempted to put out young plants until frosts have ended.
◨ CH 45cm CS 45cm Min 10°C

Matthiola incana (Stocks)
Upright spikes of flowers scent the air in late spring and early summer. The Ten Week Mixed have mainly double flowers in crimson, pink, lavender, purple and white. The Cinderella Series ♥ come in similar shades but are shorter. Grow as annuals.
◨ CH to 60cm CS to 30cm ✳✳✳

PLANTS FOR WINTER AND SPRING

You can create a year-round display using tough, reliable evergreens. Interplant them with bulbs for spring. Later, they will add structure to summer bedding.

Bulbs For crocus, *Galanthus* (snowdrops), iris, *Muscari* (grape hyacinths), narcissus, see pp.74–75; hyacinths, see left. Treat bulbs as temporary, using them for one year only and planting them in the garden, if possible, after flowering.

Brassica oleracea
(Ornamental kale)
Highly coloured ornamental kale cultivars (*see pp.8, 39*) put on a good display in autumn and through winter. Annuals, and not recommended for the table.
◨ CH and CS to 45cm ✳✳✳

Erica carnea
(Winter heath)
Evergreen heaths are good in windowboxes where you can see their winter flowers from indoors. They come in many shades of pink, purple and white; some have gold foliage. Plant in ericaceous compost.
◨ CH 15cm CS 45cm ✳✳✳

Euonymus fortunei
Evergreen shrub forming low mounds of leathery leaves, often variegated. In 'Emerald 'n' Gold' ♥ the leaves have yellow margins tinged pink in winter.
◨◧◨ CH 40cm CS 60cm ✳✳✳

HEDERA HELIX 'GOLDHEART'

Hebe pinguifolia 'Pagei' ♥
Forms neat hummocks of small blue-green leaves with spikes of white flowers in spring and summer.
◨ CH 30cm CS 90cm ✳✳✳

Hedera helix (Ivy)
Variegated ivies, with leaves marked with yellow, white or cream, brighten shaded corners. Use small-leaved ivies to trail over window-boxes, trimming regularly.
▣ CH to 3m CS indefinite ✳✳✳

Vinca minor
(Lesser periwinkle)
Evergreen, with trailing shoots studded with flowers from spring to autumn. Good for windowboxes and tall pots. Colours range from purple to pale blue and white. Look out for variegated periwinkles with cream-edged leaves. Avoid planting rampant *V. major*.
◨◧ CH 10–20cm CS 60cm ✳✳✳

Mimulus (Monkey musk)
Easily grown plants with
flowers produced throughout
late spring and summer. A
good range of bright colours,
especially yellows and reds, is
available among the bedding
mimulus. Treat these as
annuals. *M. luteus* is a
vigorous, spreading perennial
with red- or purple-spotted
yellow flowers. It is likely to
escape the container and self-
seed around the garden.
◫◫ CH 30cm CS to 60cm
❄❄❄

Nicotiana (Tobacco plant)
The flowers are often
fragrant, particularly in
evening. The Domino Series
contains attractive shades of
rose and salmon, as well as
crimson, pale green and
white. The Starship Series
stands up well to poor
weather, the plants are shorter
and good for windowboxes,
and the colour range includes
white and lime-green. Grow
as annuals, putting plants out
when frosts are over. Flowers
in light shade; the trumpets
often do not open in full sun.
◫ CH to 45cm CS to 30cm ❄

PELARGONIUM 'DOLLY VARDEN'

PETUNIA CARPET SERIES

Osteospermum
Long-flowering plant with
single daisy flowers, usually
white, pink or yellow, from
late spring to autumn above
evergreen clumps of grey-
green leaves. Flowers only
open in full sun. 'Nairobi
Purple' is short and spreading
with purple flowers, white on
the reverse and with a black
centre. 'Buttermilk' ♀ is
primrose-yellow, bronze-
tinged on the reverse with a
bluish centre. Overwinter in a
greenhouse or conservatory
or buy plantlets in spring.
◫ CH to 45cm CS to 45cm ❄

Pelargonium
One of the most traditional
plants for containers (*see
p.30*). The most suitable are
the zonal pelargoniums, often
but incorrectly known as
geraniums, such as 'Dolly
Varden' ♀ (*left*). There is a
huge range to choose from,
with flowers in shades of
pink, red, mauve, orange and
white, as well as bicolours.
Foliage may be variegated.
Trailing ivy-leaved types are
also good, especially when
planted along the edge of a

windowbox. Plants can be
protected in winter in a
greenhouse, conservatory or
unheated room.
◫ CH to 40cm CS 20–25cm
Min 2°C

Petunia
One of the most popular
annuals for every type of
container. Modern hybrids are
as fail-safe as any container
plant can be. The Carpet
Series (*left*) is compact and
spreading – flower colours
include strong reds and
purples. Double-flowered
petunias are available, and
some flowers have petals with
white stripes or margins, or
they may be heavily veined.
Wide range of small plantlets
is available in spring.
◫ CH 20–25cm CS 30–90cm
❄

Salpiglossis sinuata
Annual with heavily-veined
flowers in interesting colours,
including bronze shades, from
summer to autumn. The
Casino Series ♀ plants are
bushy and compact with good
all-weather tolerance.
◫ CH 45cm CS 30cm ❄

SALPIGLOSSIS SINUATA

SENECIO CINERARIA

Salvia
The fiery red annual *S. splendens* provides one of the brightest colours for summer bedding. 'Scarlet King' ♀ is compact and long flowering. There are many others to choose from; some with softer colours prefer light shade. The flower spikes of *S. coccinea* are not as dense.
❏❏ CH to 40cm CS to 35cm ✳

Senecio cineraria
The felted, silvery leaves of senecio make bright-flowered neighbours seem even brighter. Some plants have lacy, almost white foliage. Must have good drainage. Overwinter in a cold frame or greenhouse or buy plantlets in spring.
❏ CH 30cm CS 60cm ✳✳

Solenostemon scutellaroides
(Coleus, Painted nettle)
A foliage plant grown for its multicoloured green, cream, red and chocolate leaves. Best treated as an annual although it can be taken indoors at the end of summer and grown for longer as a pot plant. Plants in the Wizard Series are bushy and compact.
❏ CH 20cm CS to 60cm Min 4°C

Stachys byzantina (Lambs' ears)
Perennial that forms mats of woolly, silver leaves. Blends well with pink or blue flowers (*see p.36*). Its own spikes of lilac flowers appear from early summer to early autumn. A spreading plant, it would benefit from being planted out in the garden after a season in a container.
❏ CH to 45cm CS to 45cm ✳✳✳

Tagetes (French marigold)
Easily grown small annual with yellow, orange and mahogany flowers from late spring to early autumn. Leaves are aromatic, almost fern-like. The wide range available includes plenty of doubles. 'Naughty Marietta' (*below*) has single flowers.
❏ CH 30–40cm CS 30cm ✳

Tropaeolum (Nasturtium)
Colourful annual, excellent for tumbling over the edges of

TAGETES 'NAUGHTY MARIETTA'

pots and windowboxes, with flowers all summer and autumn. The Alaska Series ♀ has single flowers in orange, mahogany, yellow and cream and cream-speckled leaves. The Jewell Series has double and semi-double flowers in yellow, apricot, scarlet or crimson. 'Peach Melba' is a creamy semi-double with orange-red centres that does particularly well in containers. All are easily grown from seed which can be sown directly into the container where it is to grow. Edible leaves and flowers have a peppery taste.
❏ CH to 30cm CS to 45cm ✳

Verbena
Good for the edges of large containers; some have a spreading habit which combines well with more upright plants; others make more upright, bushy plants themselves. Flowers continue all summer and into autumn and may be scented. There is a good selection to choose from, in shades of white, peach, pink, red and purple. Protect in winter; usually grown as an annual.
❏ CH 30cm CS 30–50cm ✳

Viola (Pansy)
Familiar pansy faces come in a wide range of colours, sizes and markings. Perennial but usually grown as an annual or biennial. Blooms in sun or part shade but plants last longer out of hot summer sun. Winter-flowering pansies need plenty of light if they are to bloom through the season. Deadhead regularly.
❏❏ CH to 25cm CS to 30cm ✳✳✳

ROCK PLANTS FOR TROUGHS

Most rock plants need a free-draining compost (*see p.55*). A top-dressing of coarse grit helps to protect stems and lower leaves from rotting or being splashed by compost. Choose plants that have similar requirements for sun or shade, and be ready to divide any that display an invasive tendency.

ANDROSACE CARNEA SUBSP. LAGGERI

Acaena (New Zealand burr)
Low, creeping evergreen perennials with dainty filigree foliage. 'Blue Haze' (*see p.53*) has blue-grey leaves with round, rust-coloured burrs in mid to late summer. *A. microphylla* is smaller-growing; some plants have bronze leaves.
❑ CH to 15cm CS 30cm ✱✱✱

Achillea × lewisii 'King Edward' ♀
Flat lemon flowerheads top mats of soft, ferny, grey-green leaves from early to mid-summer (*see p.53*).
❑ CH 8–12cm CS 25cm ✱✱✱

Androsace carnea
(Rock jasmine)
An evergreen rock plant ideal for placing at the edge of a trough or sink. Clusters of small pink flowers form above rosettes of leaves in late spring. Subspecies *laggeri* has loose heads of deep pink flowers. Good drainage is essential.
❑ CH 5cm CS 8–15cm ✱✱✱

Arenaria balearica
A creeping perennial with tiny, shining evergreen leaves that form tight mats. Small star-shaped white flowers emerge at random throughout the summer. Ideal as a miniature alpine lawn in a trough in a shaded site.
❑ CH 1–2cm CS 30cm ✱✱✱

Artemisia schmidtiana
'Nana' ♀
Grow in a sunny trough where it will make a silver carpet of fine silky leaves. An evergreen perennial that needs good drainage; add extra grit to the potting compost.
❑ CH 8cm CS 30cm ✱✱✱

Campanula (Bellflower)
Many of the small campanulas are suitable for troughs. The flowers, usually blue but sometimes white or lilac, appear in summer. *C. poscharskyana* has small blue bells and forms evergreen mats of bright green leaves; invasive and may need regular dividing. *C. raineri* is tiny and low-growing; it succeeds in shade. *C. carpatica* var. *turbinata* has fairly large upturned bells; 'Jewel' (*see p.53*) is compact with purple-blue flowers. Deadheading is needed to prevent faded, brown flowers from marring the display. A top-dressing of grit helps to protect against slugs.
❑❑ CH to 15cm CS 30–45cm ✱✱✱

Crocus
The familiar harbingers of early spring with their goblet-shaped flowers. These need sun to open. *C. chrysanthus* types, such as 'Gipsy Girl' (*below*) are generally suitable for troughs with free-draining compost. 'Snow Bunting' ♀ is creamy-white with pale grey feathering; 'Cream Beauty' ♀ is fragrant, and 'E.A. Bowles' ♀ is lemon with a bronze-green base.
❑ CH 7cm CS 5cm ✱✱✱

CROCUS 'GIPSY GIRL'

CYCLAMEN COUM PEWTER GROUP

Cyclamen

The delightful white, pink and carmine flowers of *C. coum* ♀ appear in late winter and early spring. The leaves, sometimes strikingly marked with silver patterns, can be almost as attractive as the flowers. The Pewter Group ♀ have almost entirely silver leaves. *C. hederifolium* ♀ flowers in autumn and can also have well-marked leaves. Cyclamen need gritty compost, with leaf mould or garden compost added, if possible. Plant tubers shallowly, almost on the compost's surface.
◘ CH 5–8cm CS 10cm ✳✳✳

Galanthus nivalis

(Snowdrop)
Charming late winter or early spring flowers for a natural-looking planting in partial shade. A raised trough enables you to appreciate them without getting on hands and knees. There are many with single flowers, but the double 'Flore Pleno' ♀ is easy to grow. Split clumps just after flowering, if necessary.
◘ CH 5–8cm CS 5–6cm ✳✳✳

Gentiana sino-ornata ♀

Brilliant blue trumpets give colour from autumn into early winter. 'Kingfisher' (*below*) is similar. Plant in ericaceous compost. One of the easiest gentians to grow.
◘ CH 5–7cm CS 15–30 cm ✳✳✳

Helianthemum (Rock rose)

Will bring colour to troughs in the sun, with flowers in white, shades of pink, red or yellow, and silvery foliage. A spreading evergreen, it will trail over a trough's sides; some plants can be upright.
◘ CH to 30cm CS to 30cm ✳✳✳

Iberis sempervirens

(Perennial candytuft)
A particularly good scrambler for covering the sides of large troughs. The dark evergreen leaves make a useful mat of foliage all year. In late spring, the plant is covered by masses of small white flowers.
◘ CH 30cm CS to 40cm ✳✳✳

Iris histrioides

A small bulbous iris with mid- to dark blue flowers in

GENTIANA 'KINGFISHER'

NARCISSUS BULBOCODIUM

early spring. Ideal in a raised alpine trough where the full beauty of the flowers can be appreciated more easily; could also be grown in a window-box. Keep as dry as possible in summer.
◘ CH 10–15cm CS 5cm ✳✳✳

Muscari armeniacum ♀

(Grape hyacinth)
Easily grown bulb with short, dense spikes of tiny round blue bells in spring. Good in a large container or trough. Can produce a lot of foliage; if this becomes messy as the season wears on, it can be trimmed, unlike that of other bulbs, without detriment to the plant. Self-seeds readily.
◘ CH 20cm CS 8cm ✳✳✳

Narcissus bulbocodium ♀

(Hoop petticoat daffodil)
A small group of these delicate flowers (*above*) makes a charming addition to an alpine trough. The funnel-shaped trumpets are produced in spring. Grow in a sunny sheltered spot where the flowers will not be damaged by wind.
◘ CH 10–15cm CS 5cm ✳✳✳

ORIGANUM 'KENT BEAUTY'

Origanum 'Kent Beauty'
One of several decorative types of marjoram grown for their charming pink or green flowerheads. These will spill over the side of a trough from mid- to late summer. Leaves are aromatic but not edible. Other decorative marjorams include *O. amanum* ♥ and the more upright, purple-pink *O. laevigatum* ♥. All need good drainage and will not survive excessively wet winter conditions combined with cold. Protect with a propped piece of glass, if possible.
◧ CH 10–20cm CS to 30cm ✳✳✳

Oxalis adenophylla ♥
A delicate-looking perennial with grey-green leaves and purplish-pink flowers in late spring. Flowers only open in good light. Can be tricky.
◧ CH 10cm CS to 15cm ✳✳✳

Primula auricula ♥
(Auricula)
Clusters of flowers, often with contrasting eyes or rings of white or gold, appear in late spring above evergreen rosettes of leaves (*see p.49*).

Flower colours include purple, red, blue, green and yellow. Sometimes petals and leaves have a floury dusting. Add leaf mould or garden compost to a gritty planting compost.
◧ CH 20cm CS 25cm ✳✳✳

Saxifraga (Saxifrage)
Wide range of alpine plants, often forming mats of foliage. The flowers in spring come in delicate shades of pink, lemon and white. For a challenge, try 'Tumbling Waters' ♥, with silvery-green leaves powdered white and clusters of white flowers; 'Southside Seedling' ♥ has sprays of tiny pink and white flowers; *S. burseriana* has lemon flowers and needs protection from very hot sun. Use gritty compost and top-dress with coarse grit.
◧ CH 45cm CS 30cm ✳✳✳

Scutellaria indica var. **parvifolia** (Skullcap)
Although it tolerates sun, a useful plant for a large alpine trough that is in partial shade. Lavender-blue tubular flowers are borne in summer above tufts of silver-grey leaves.
◧ CH 25cm CS 30cm ✳✳✳

OXALIS ADENOPHYLLA

SEMPERVIVUM TECTORUM

Sedum spathulifolium
An easily grown succulent with tiny rosettes of fleshy grey-green leaves, sometimes tinted purple. Spreads to form mats of foliage covered with bright yellow flowers in summer. 'Cape Blanco' ♥ (*see p.53*) has leaves heavily powdered with white. The leaves of 'Purpureum' ♥ have rich purple tones.
◧ CH 10cm CS 60cm ✳✳✳

Sempervivum tectorum
(Houseleek)
Rosettes of succulent green, blue-green or red-purple leaves make neat mats. Upright flowers shoot from their centre in summer. Plants thrive in poor conditions.
◧ CH 15cm CS to 50cm ✳✳✳

Thymus (Thyme)
Low-growing thymes make attractive, aromatic trough plants. 'Doone Valley' forms mats of olive-green leaves splashed yellow, covered in summer with lavender-pink flowers. 'Silver Posie' makes a miniature bush with white-edged leaves. There are also gold-leaved thymes. All can be used in cooking, although plain green common thyme has the best flavour.
◧ CH to 20cm CS to 35cm ✳✳✳

EDIBLE PLANTS

Most herbs make excellent container plants for the patio or windowsill. Vegetables and fruit need care with watering and feeding. Crops will be small but can be picked at the peak of freshness. Choose dwarf, fast-maturing vegetable cultivars and feed with a quick-acting liquid fertilizer.

FRUIT AND VEGETABLES

Beans
Grow dwarf French beans such as 'Delinel', putting 4 plants to a deep 30cm pot. Runner beans can be put in half-barrels, trained up a wigwam of 1.8m canes. Keep well fed and watered.

Carrots
Feathery foliage is attractive in windowboxes. Choose stump-rooted types.

Chillies
Need a really sunny, sheltered spot and long season to ripen. Several types available, imbuing dishes with varying degrees of heat. 'Apache' makes a small, compact plant.

Lettuce
The frilly leaves of 'Lollo Rossa' (right) and 'Salad Bowl' types are decorative and can be picked a few at a time. Keep well watered and out of full sun.

Tomatoes
Give tomatoes in containers a sunny, sheltered site where they will develop most flavour. Trailing 'Tumbler' is good in windowboxes.

Strawberries
Containers can produce a good crop in a sunny spot. Water well when fruit is swelling and feed every 2 weeks with a high-potash fertilizer. Replace plants every 2 years. Alpine strawberries are good in windowboxes and do well in light shade.

Citrus See p.65

HERBS

Basil
A tender annual that does especially well in pots in a warm, sheltered corner or on a sill. Pinch out shoot tips regularly to prevent plants becoming lanky, and keep on the dry side.
◨ CH 30–60cm CS 30cm ✳

Chives
Easy to grow in sun or part shade. The mauve pompon flowers are an added attraction in early summer.
◨◨ CH to 60cm CS 5cm ✳✳✳

Marjoram
Stems of aromatic leaves are topped by pretty pink flowers in early summer. 'Aureum' has yellow leaves.
◨ CH 30cm CS 30cm ✳✳✳

Mint
Invasive and best grown in its own pot. Various types have subtly differing flavours; those with variegated leaves often make more compact plants. Grows in shade and needs moisture.
◨◈ CH to 60cm CS indefinite ✳✳✳

Parsley
The curly-leaved type is ornamental but the flat-leaved type has a better flavour. Grow as an annual.
◨◨ CH 30cm CS 30cm ✳✳✳

Sage
Gold- and purple-leaved sages taste good and look attractive mixed with other plants. Trim after flowering or in early spring to keep in shape.
◨ CH 45cm CS 60cm ✳✳✳

See also **Thyme** (*opposite*) and **Bay** and **Rosemary** (*pp.66–67*).

LETTUCE 'LOLLO ROSSA'

INDEX

Page numbers in *italics* indicate illustrations.

ACKNOWLEDGMENTS

Picture research Christine Rista

Special photography Peter Anderson

Illustrations Karen Cochrane

Index Hilary Bird

Dorling Kindersley would like to thank:
All staff at the RHS, in particular Susanne
Mitchell, Karen Wilson and Barbara Haynes
at Vincent Square; Gerry Adamson for advice
and assistance with the woodwork projects;
Cuprinol Ltd (for wood preservative, p.33);
Rein Ltd (for reinforcing fibres used in the
cement trough, p.52); Stanley Tools Ltd.

The Royal Horticultural Society
To learn more about the work of the
Society, visit the RHS on the Internet at
www.rhs.org.uk. Information includes news of
events around the country, a horticultural
database, international plant registers, results
of plant trials and membership details.

Photography
The publisher would also like to thank the
following for their kind permission to
reproduce their photographs:
(key: t=top, c=centre, b=below, l=left, r=right)

DK Special Photography: Dave King 58bc
The Garden Picture Library: Linda Burgess
24; Mayer/ Le Scanff 6; J. S. Sira 11t;
Friedrich Strauss 22br
John Glover: jacket back tc, 4bl, 5bl, 7, 9t,
10, 12l, 17, 21t, 22tr, 47b, designer Mark
Anthony Walker
Harpur Garden Library: jacket back c;
designer Martin Sacks 9b; designer Simon
Fraser 12r
Andrew Lawson: jacket front tl and lct, 2, 8l,
11b, 14bl, 15br, 16, 19tr, 20
Clive Nichols Garden Pictures: jacket front r;
19br; Chenies Manor, Buckinghamshire 13b;
Keukenhof, Holland 19tl; South View
Nurseries, Hampshire 8r; Graham Strong 18
Photo Lamontagne: 30